D0897099

For Cori, Adam, Derek, Natasha,
and that enigma of noir,
Shadow.

Acknowledgments

Books like this involve a great many folks who help out in ways too numerous and varied to mention. Still, I like to take a stab at including everyone, although invariably I forget someone, and the omission usually leads to a deep-seated and lifelong resentment of me that is as unshakable as the belief that law-enforcement officials prefer dough-nuts as a daily snack. The most important person to thank is Kathy Simpson, who not only does an excellent job editing, but also manages to tolerate my eccentricities without having to seek out a prescription for tranquilizers. Also at Peachpit, I need to thank Cliff Colby, Rebecca Ross, Tracey Croom, David Van Ness, and Julie Bess for their various roles in bringing this book to market.

In the podcasting world, I need to thank (in no particular order) Phil Torrone, Swoopy, Evo Terra, Richard Lucic, Jason Litchford, Sharon Housley, Eric Boyer, Chris McIntyre, Brandon Fuller, Bob Goyetche, August Trometer, Aaron Price, Ben Williams, Greg Kaufman, Tod Maffin, Chris Breen, Greg Pool, Michael Mennenga, Elizabeth Tracey, and Dr. Rick Lange, M.D. I'd like to single out Steve Mirsky for putting up with the fact that I made a rookie mistake when recording our conversation, which forced us to cover the interview twice. I'll never live it down.

Last, I'd like to thank Jen Gareau; Jeff Govier; Lance Campbell; Chris McVeigh; and my parents, Glen Farkas and Lu Farkas (specifically for their babysitting assistance).

Table of Contents

Chapter 3   Creating a Podcast 87

Chapter 4   Video Podcasting 167

Foreword

I'm not sure what it is about Bart Farkas and forewords, but the last time I penned one of these things, it was in the guise of Michel Nostradamus, the 16th century's all-seeing, dyspeptic monk, in the first pages of Bart's and my book, *The Macintosh Bible Guide to Games*. Rib-tickling as that foreword was, we sold something like a baker's dozen worth of the book. Given *TMBGtG*'s less-than-stellar sales, I'm shocked that Bart would risk opening this book with yet another inane foreword penned by yours truly.

Ah, well, such is the ill-considered good nature of your typical Canadian.

The difference between that book and this one, of course, is that—unbeknownst to us at the time—computer gaming was on the wane, whereas the subject of this book has barely begun its assured meteoric rise. With Bart's *Secrets of Podcasting,* you're getting in on the ground floor of the electrifying new technology known as podcasting.

The author will go into greater detail on the subject, but allow me to dip my oar in as well and say that podcasting is A Big Deal. It's going to profoundly change the way you consume news and entertainment, as well as give a voice to those who normally work well outside the bounds of tra-ditional media. Follow the techniques in this book, and one of those voices may even be yours.

One of the benefits of writing forewords is that you have the opportunity to read the book while it's still *in utero*—long before some befuddled crank on Amazon issues a one-star rating because he's disappointed that the book fails to address the intimate workings of Orvis's Vortex VO2 Fly Reel. I've taken the time to read the book, and I assure you, you're getting the goods. Not only does Bart clearly show you how to bring podcasts into your life (and onto your computer and portable music player), but he also tells you all you need to know to create a quality (and, one hopes, *compelling*) podcast of your own. Along the way, he speaks with individuals who are creating today's best podcasts and passing along their insights on how to do it right.

You're in good hands. Enjoy the book. Discover podcasts that stir you. And if the spirit moves you, make some of your own.

I'll be listening.

—**Christopher Breen**
Editor in chief, Playlistmag.com
Author of *Secrets of the iPod and iTunes*

Podcasting Basics

Wouldn't it be nice to be able to listen to radio programs, audiobooks and magazines, and alternative broadcasting on your *own* time? Heck, it might even be nice to make your very own broadcasts that others could listen to and enjoy. If you have ever been interested in such a concept, the wait is over. In fact, the wait has been over for a little more than a year now, but the speed at which podcasting is becoming entrenched as a legitimate broadcast medium and the unbelievable rate of its evolution make it seem like podcasting has been around a lot longer than it really has.

The revolution continues, and it's not just gaining steam; it's beginning to steamroll other forms of information delivery, causing large ripples in the ponds of radio, television, and even publishing. Podcasting, as it has become known, is a new and exciting form of Web-based (that's World Wide Web–based) broadcasting. This chapter takes a look at just what podcasting is, where it came from, and what effect it has had on media distribution and the public's listening habits since its creation.

What Is Podcasting?

In a nutshell, *podcasting* is a World Wide Web–based form of broadcasting that allows anyone with a computer and/or a digital media device to download and listen to content. Formed by the combination of the words *iPod* and *broadcasting,* podcasting involves the creation of "radio" shows that are not intended to be broadcast over Marconi's invention. Indeed, these podcasts can be downloaded and enjoyed only through access to the World Wide Web. Podcasts can be enjoyed via a media player on your computer (such as RealPlayer or Windows Media Player), or they can be uploaded directly to your digital media device (such as an iPod) for enjoyment any time and anywhere.

Recently, a new kind of podcast has arisen: video podcasting (or, as it's sometimes called, vodcasting). Video podcasting was around in the early days, but video podcasts could be viewed only on home computers using Windows Media Player or QuickTime (or similar software). With the release of Apple's very popular video iPod, however, as well as Creative's Zen Vision, the floodgates were opened for video podcasts, and as a result, an increasing number of podcasts are being produced as video content. This shift has already altered the podcasting landscape significantly, pushing some podcast creators to make video versions of their podcasts to complement their standard audio content.

Over the past few years, sales of digital music, photo, and digital video devices such as Apple's iPod line, MP3 players, and even cell phones and Palm Pilots have been soaring to new heights. Indeed, these devices have been finding their way into the pockets and purses of a wide cross-section of the North American public. With these gadgets becoming increasingly cosmopolitan, it was perhaps inevitable that a mass movement away from standard media broadcast methods would occur. After all, what's on the radio might not be what the customer wants to hear at any given time, and the majority of digital media devices don't even have built-in radios. Enter the podcast.

The concept is simplicity itself: Allow users to listen to (or watch) exactly *what* they want, *when* they want, and *where* they want. With today's world becoming progressively crammed with tasks ranging from doing the dishes to taking the kids to karate class, the ability to time-shift information is increasingly desirable. On the other side of the coin are the folks who want to produce podcasts. With little more than a computer, a microphone, and some freeware (or shareware), anyone can produce an audio podcast on any topic under the sun. Producing a video podcast requires a little more gumption, but not so much that any Joe Blow can't create one in the confines of his den or office.

It's a new medium, to be sure, and it is still in its formative years, but podcasting and its variants are here to stay. From large corporations looking for new ways to get their programs heard or their ideas across, to home-brewed shows covering diverse topics ranging from sports to wine tasting to marital issues and beyond, podcasting is proving that it has the power and flexibility to reshape the media landscape. As the Web site Podcast Alley (**Figure 1.1**) says, "Free the Airwaves!"

Figure 1.1

Podcast Alley (www. podcastalley.com) is one of the best places to look for the hottest podcasts of all shapes and sizes.

How It Works

The cutting edge of podcasting involves a set of rules known as *RSS (Really Simple Syndication)*. RSS allows podcast content to be syndicated instantly on the World Wide Web for download and use by anyone who has an interest in listening to it (or watching it, in the case of video podcasts). By using RSS, the creator of a podcast can make his or her material available to anyone in the world (who has access to the Internet) within a matter of minutes.

With the evolution of RSS and associated technologies, podcasting becomes analogous to a TiVo for audio broadcasts of all kinds. Once syndicated, a podcast is disseminated over the World Wide Web to anyone who has subscribed to that content. Via RSS, podcasts are downloaded to a user's computer and can be uploaded to a digital media player the next time it is connected to the computer. Soon, digital media players will have wireless connectivity, allowing podcast content to be streamed to these players in much the same way that laptop computers connect to wireless networks in airports and coffee shops the world over.

Although this process may sound complicated and cumbersome, it really isn't. Thanks to incredibly versatile and user-friendly software like Apple's iTunes, iPodder, and video-specific programs like TVTonic (**Figure 1.2**), the process of enjoying podcasts plays out like a soft Jamaican breeze.

Although syndication is probably the most popular way of obtaining podcasts, there are other ways to get your hands on these audio and video gems without committing to daily or weekly content. Many podcasts are available as one-time downloads or as streaming content from podcasting Web sites (the number of which is sure to mushroom even while this book is at the printer), giving you the option of sampling small bites rather than ordering a four-course meal.

Technically speaking, any media event that is played on a digital media device such as an iPod or other MP3 player is a podcast. Indeed, many weekly magazines, radio shows, and even television shows (such as "The Charlie Rose Show") are available for download in MP3 format for use on digital media devices or home computers. As one might expect, many of these commercial ventures are associated with some small cost, but that is just one small area of the podcasting realm. In fact,

Figure 1.2

TVTonic is a Windows-only, Web-based video podcast aggregator that allows you to manage all your video podcasts easily in one handy location.

99 percent of all podcast content has no cost associated with it other than the necessary audio hardware and computer/Internet connection.

Why Podcast?

The answer to the above question is simple: Podcasting is so incredibly simple, especially compared with getting your own FCC license, that virtually anyone with a personal computer and an Internet connection can produce a show that could potentially be heard by tens of thousands of people. In the United States alone, where freedom of speech is set forth as one of the founding pillars of society, one does not have to take a large leap of faith to imagine that the podwaves are filling with interesting, offensive, humorous, and often inane chatter.

You may ask, "Who is podcasting?" That question can be answered very simply: Everyone is podcasting. **Figure 1.3**, for example, shows the conversational portion of a musical podcast from Tree House Concerts (see the interview with Tree House Concerts in Chapter 3). By *everyone,* I mean people from all geographic locations and all walks of life, and that number is growing by leaps and bounds. Between the first and second editions of this book, the number of podcasts available more than doubled.

Figure 1.3

A preperformance podcast interview in progress at Tree House Concerts (www.treehouse concerts.org).

Photo courtesy of Tree House Concerts

If the Internet ushered in a revolution in information dissemination, podcasting has done the same for the audio and video formats. Podcasting is the metaphorical saw that cuts through the chains of radio and television, be they satellite radio, old-fashioned AM/FM radio broadcasts, or network television stations.

The following is a short list of the sorts of topics that are routinely discussed in podcasts available today:

- Wine connoisseurship

- Husband-and-wife relationships

- Suburban life

- Macintosh technical issues

- Geek news

- Science fiction

- Comedy

- How-to shows

- Sports

- Skepticism

- UFOs

- Music shows of all genres

Needless to say, this list could go on and on. And on. The number of podcasts is growing exponentially, and by the time you read this book, there likely will be a podcast for nearly every subject that could come to mind (if there isn't already). If you can think of a subject that isn't covered, you've found your niche to start podcasting in yourself!

Commercial Podcasting

For existing radio networks, individual radio stations, and even television stations, the move to podcasting is an obvious one. These outlets quickly realized that there was a market for their programming to be disseminated in the form of MP3 or AAC files for audio, and MP4 or QuickTime files for video, so that individuals could enjoy them on their own time. And while the listener/viewer has control over whether she listens to or watches any advertisements during the program, the exposure can only serve to aid in the growth of a fan base for any program. As a result, an increasing number of media outlets are making podcasts available to the public from their Web sites. A trip to ESPN's Web site, for example, shows an area specifically for podcasts (**Figure 1.4**).

Figure 1.4

Most Web sites now include specific areas for podcasting.

Also, several Web sites, including Apple Computer's iTunes Music Store and Audible.com's online store (**Figure 1.5**), sell commercial podcasts of periodicals such as *Scientific American* magazine and newspapers such as *The Wall Street Journal*. The cost of these podcasts is often less than that of the publications on the newsstand, and they can be purchased through subscription, much like any magazine or newspaper. As time goes on, we can expect nearly every magazine to be available in this format, allowing readers everywhere to get in their reading while riding a bike or driving a car.

Figure 1.5

Audible.com's Web site sells audiobooks and also commercial podcasts of popular television and radio shows.

The Podcasting Echo

Exactly what mark podcasting will make on the world is a chapter that is as yet unwritten, although it's clear that podcasting is here to stay. Still, despite the fact that podcasting is in its infancy, we don't need a crystal ball to see that the whirlwind surrounding it today will most likely stir up the sand in several established sandboxes. Let's take a look at what areas are being affected, directly or indirectly, by the rise of podcasting:

Conventional radio. Perhaps the one area that might be most affected by podcasting, traditional radio has a lot to lose. In today's world, most of the people who listen to radio do so in their cars. With an increasing number of cars coming with MP3 players or Apple iPod connections, the ability for a driver to listen to podcast material rather than advertisement-laden radio broadcasts is on the increase. The effects of this on radio are already apparent, with many radio programs offering podcast versions of their shows via station Web sites.

note
There are also products on the market that effectively turn any radio broadcast into a podcast. Griffin Technology's radio SHARK (www.griffintechnology.com), for example, will capture any AM or FM radio broadcast and automatically export an MP3 file to iTunes so that the program will be loaded directly onto your iPod the next time you connect it to your computer.

Satellite radio. With less to lose than conventional radio (because satellite radio doesn't include advertising), satellite radio is still in a flat position because its content is available only at set times. Podcasts are available at any time. It's clear that satellite radio providers have seen the podcasting revolution coming and that they are taking steps to embrace podcasting, rather than rallying the troops to fight it. Sirius Satellite Radio, in fact, hired Adam Curry to do a new show called "Adam Curry's PodShow" on its network (although Curry still creates his usual podcast, "The Daily Dose"). Sirius also has a special Web page, Sirius Podcast Central (**Figure 1.6**), featuring various Sirius shows that are available in podcast format.

Figure 1.6

Sirius Satellite Radio has a special Web page to go along with its podcast guru show, "Adam Curry's PodShow."

Internet radio. Internet radio is perhaps the safest of the radio media because software already exists that allows the user to time-shift Internet radio shows. The downside to Internet radio is that it is primarily intended to be listened to on a computer and, as such, doesn't have the mobility of a podcast.

Celebrity. In less than a year of official existence, the podcast has already created celebrity. Of course, Curry (former MTV veejay) is the face of iPodder and podcasting in general, but the hosts of the most popular podcasts are also beginning to achieve some measure of celebrity—Dawn Miceli and Drew Domkus of "The Dawn and Drew Show," for example. It's only a matter of time before a podcaster makes the jump from podcasting to mainstream popularity on television or in network radio. Indeed, Curry has already done that with his deal on Sirius Satellite Radio, but he was already a celebrity of sorts before getting into podcasting.

Television. In the early days, television didn't have a great deal to fear from podcasting, but those days are past. With the significant sales of video-based digital media players, and with Apple's inclusion of network television shows in the iTunes Music Store, television has been thrust into the podcasting realm whether it likes it or not. As of this writing, the video podcasting experiment has been a huge success, and Apple is constantly adding television content to its store for those with video iPods (or those who like to watch in iTunes on their home computers) to enjoy. Apple sells network television shows for $1.99 per episode and now offers a Season Pass option for an entire season of a show at a discounted rate. Talk-based shows like "The Charlie Rose Show" and "BBC News Hour" are available on commercial services like Audible.com (www.audible.com), but increasingly, television shows are being offered for those with the capability of watching them on portable media devices.

A Tiny Screen: Is It Worth It?

The video iPod (**Figure 1.7**) has a 2.5-inch screen. I own one of these, and the question I'm most frequently asked is "Can you even watch a show with a screen that small?" The answer is a qualified "Yes." This is not the way you want to watch television or movies on a regular basis, but when you find out that your flight is canceled, and there is going to be yet another 3-hour layover in a depressing airport somewhere, being able to pull out a video

 iPod (or other such device) and watch a few episodes of a favorite TV show is a welcome ability. Sure, the screen is small, but you get used to it very quickly, and you forget the size of the screen as the show pulls you in.

Figure 1.7
Video iPods offer users the ability to watch television shows right on their iPods for a nominal cost.

Advertising. The obvious problem for advertisers lies in placing advertising in a medium that prides itself on freedom: freedom of ideas, freedom from advertisers' pressure, freedom to say what they want. With podcasting's increasing fan base, you can be sure that corporations will want to find a way to advertise, but it's unclear whether the listeners will accept such a thing. Perhaps the most logical path will be for companies to sponsor the production of individual podcasts, thus attaching their names to successful podcasting endeavors.

Education. Although at one time, this concept was highly speculative, that speculation has become reality as university classes are increasingly digitally recorded and then made available on a Web site as podcast "notes." Students can download the audio of that class and listen to it while they're out drinking beer and eating pizza later that evening. The possibilities for education are huge, and as MP3 players and iPods become ubiquitous (in phones and PDAs, and as stand-alone players), the ability for education to take advantage of this information pathway is increased. As mentioned in Chapter 2, Duke University has embraced podcasting technology, so who knows what the future of education will be as it pertains to podcasting?

Book and magazine publishers. Perhaps at the forefront of podcasting (although some would argue that pay service isn't true podcasting), Audible.com went online in late 1997 and was at the forefront of digital audio content delivery. Audible made its name by selling audiobooks for use on the computer, CD player, or MP3 player, but since its inception, it has been on the cutting edge, offering everything from comedy shows to daily newspapers (in audio format). No doubt the success of Audible.com has spurred more publishers to produce audio versions of their books, thus changing the publishing landscape.

The legal system. Any time there is talk of digital content of any kind, legal ramifications start to rear their ugly heads. Although independent podcasts are free to the world, it's only a matter of time before some conflict arises in this area. How and when are matters of opinion, but one has only to look at the music industry to see how ugly things can become. That said, let's try to be optimistic. Perhaps the spirit of podcasting will prevail, and the medium will thrive without copyright-infringement lawsuits to bog it down.

Commerce. As mentioned previously, Web sites like Audible.com and Apple's iTunes Music Store already sell what are essentially podcast versions of popular radio and television shows, as well as audio versions of periodicals. As podcasting continues to take off, one can imagine compact discs for sale with hundreds of podcasts in a sort of "Best of Podcasting 2006" compilation. No doubt we will see many changes in commerce and e-commerce as a result of podcasting's entrance into the marketplace.

A Brief History of Podcasting

How can I write a history of something that has been around for just over a year? The answer to that question lies in the truism that just about nothing is created in a vacuum, and just as x-ray photography evolved from radiation tests, podcasting evolved from humbler beginnings. Podcasting's roots actually are planted in the world of blogs (Web logs). Therefore, we must look first at the origin of the blog. Indeed, to see the genesis of podcasting, we have to go back—way back—to the mist-shrouded days of the 1980s.

note

What is a blog? A *blog*, or *Web log*, is a World Wide Web page where content is added periodically and time- and date-stamped. These additions can be made by one or more people, including the general public. The content of a blog can range from diary entries to news items to opinions on world events. Today, some blogs contain links to podcasts—which isn't surprising, considering that the roots of podcasting are firmly planted in blog soil. As an aside, the Merriam-Webster dictionary announced that by virtue of the number of online lookups, *blog* received its "Word of the Year" award in 2004. (For some reason, *defenestration* made No. 10 on the list.)

The home computer and Internet

Entire phone book–size books have been written about the history of the home computer and the Internet, and I'm pretty sure that you don't want me to go down that road in a book about podcasting! That said, I'll cut to the chase and just say that the current ubiquity of the home computer and nearly universal access to the Internet (in one form or another) are the structural underpinnings that make podcasting possible to begin with. Without this technology in millions of homes, this book wouldn't have been written. 'Nuff said.

The blog

While some people feel that the roots of blogging lie in the ashes of pen-pal relationships and ham-radio operation, let's start with the computer culture of the 1980s. By the early '80s, the personal computer was starting to take hold. Apple was still king (in terms of home computers), but others, such as IBM and Commodore, were making significant inroads as the years passed. By mid-decade, many computer users had modems, and they were using these modems to log on to bulletin boards (also known as *BBs*), e-mail lists, or online services such as GEnie and CompuServe (precursors of today's AOL). Many aspects of these outlets and services were essentially early versions of Web logs. People could dial in with their modems, read new messages that had been posted by others, and then enter their own messages.

Clearly, the seeds of blogging were sown in the 1980s, but the real sprouting and growth of blogging occurred in the mid-1990s, paralleling the meteoric rise of the Internet and the World Wide Web. According to Wikipedia, the term *Web log* was coined in 1997 by Weblog pioneer Jorn Barger. By the eve of the turn of the century, *Web log* had melded into the single word *blog*, and the popularity of blogs started to skyrocket. Ultimately, a gentleman by the name of Dave Winer designed a way to inform users when their favorite blogs had been updated with new information, thus making blogging even more versatile and useful to the masses. Today, there are countless blogs, many of which have large followings, such as Jade Walker's The Blog of Death, shown in **Figure 1.8**.

Figure 1.8

www.blogofdeath.com, the brainchild of Jade Walker, is typical of the modern blog. The Blog of Death is a very popular site for those interested in detailed obituaries of unique individuals who had an impact on our world.

Audio blogging

Audio blogging was a variant of the blog that involved the posting of audio files rather than text in its entries. By all accounts, the audio blog was not a resounding success in terms of garnering the kind of world-wide attention that the blog had. Still, the audio blog existed, and files were usually offered in MP3 format, although occasionally, other Web-based formats, like Flash (Macromedia), would be used. It was from the underpinnings of audio blogging that podcasting arose.

In 2004, the RSS format was combined with aggregator software, essentially to check RSS-enabled Web pages for new audio content and keep users up to date on content. In English, that means that a combination of software programs came together to enable people to subscribe easily to audio content (podcasts) and have that content delivered directly to their home computers and, ultimately, their digital media devices (MP3 players).

The digital media player

With all the talk about Web logs, blogging, and audio blogging, it can be easy to forget that the digital media player, otherwise known as an MP3 player (**Figure 1.9**) or iPod (**Figure 1.10**), also played a key role in the sudden rise and popularity of podcasting. The lineage of today's digital media players can be traced back to the venerable Sony Walkman from the late '70s. A play-only cassette tape machine, the Walkman was small enough that it could be taken virtually anywhere, and it became a huge hit, selling around 3 million units in its first 3 years of sales. (By comparison, Apple has moved more than triple that amount of iPods in a similar timeframe.)

Figure 1.9

A Samsung YP-Z5 MP3 player.

From the Walkman sprouted plenty of competition, including cassette tape players with radios included. These devices ultimately shrank to near the size of the cassette tapes themselves. In the mid-1980s, the compact disc (CD) hit the market and took it by storm. It wasn't long before portable CD players showed up, and these, too, progressed from relatively bulky devices to very slim and elegant designs that were not much larger than the CDs themselves.

Figure 1.10

Apple's iPods, like this iPod nano, have taken the world by storm, capturing the vast majority of the market.

Photo courtesy of Apple Computer, Inc

By 1998, the MP3 format was being used to play music on computers (with the help of a piece of software called WinAmp), and during that same year, the first viable MP3 player emerged on the market. Early MP3 players were flash memory–based (meaning that they had a small, fixed amount of space to hold music), but by late 1999, hard drive–based MP3 players also started to appear. The market for MP3 players was very fragmented until Apple Computer released the first iPod in October 2001.

The iPod has been nothing short of a resounding success, and in the few short years since the iPod's introduction, Apple has gained control of more than 90 percent of the hard drive–based player market and

80 percent of the total MP3 player market. With Apple's dominance and cultural influence with regard to MP3 players, it's no wonder that the term *podcasting* includes a reference to the iPod.

MP3 players today include software that makes moving music and other audio files from the Internet to computer to player very simple. Apple's iTunes software significantly affected the simplicity of all vendors' software in this manner, making podcasting easier for the average user. In the past few months, several companies (including Apple and Creative) have released video-capable digital media devices. In Apple's case, the device was the video iPod, while Creative introduced the Zen Vision. Both of these products are excellent and allow users to watch video wherever they want. With the huge success of video in the iTunes Music Store, we can expect to see plenty more video-ready digital media players hitting the market in the coming year.

The MP3 file

The MP3 file was developed in Germany by Dieter Seitzer and Karlheinz Brandenburg at a company called Fraunhofer-Gesellschaft and at the University of Erlangen. The *MP* part of *MP3* refers to the MPEG roots of MP3 compression. *MPEG* stands for *Moving Picture Experts Group*, which was established in 1988 to set standards for digital encoding. Developed and perfected in the mid-1990s, the *MP3* format, which stands for *MPEG Audio Layer 3*, became the standard for digital audio compression worldwide.

MP3 compression is necessary because CD-quality audio files are extremely large—too large, in fact, to fit on digital players of the day. An average song on a CD might consist of 30 MB to 40 MB of information, while that same song in MP3 format could be whittled down nearly tenfold—to 3.5 MB or 4 MB—with minimal quality loss. Obviously, without the MP3 format, the rise of small digital media devices would have been cost prohibitive and unrealistic.

As another piece of the puzzle, the MP3 format is one of the key elements of the rise of the podcasting phenomenon (among many other things). Although the MP3 format has been eclipsed by AAC (the format Apple uses on its iPods), it is still a viable and frequently used compression method for all Web-based audio content.

The MP4 file

The MP4 format (MPEG-4, for *Moving Pictures Expert Group*-4) was introduced in 1998. MP4 incorporates various portions of other MPEG standards and is designed specifically for video playback. MP4 files are the standard files for such players as Apple's video iPod, Creative's Zen Vision:M, and iRiver's U10. The MP4 format allows for creating video files for portable video players, for burning files onto CD-ROM for home computer use, and also for streaming files over the Internet. In short, the MP4 format is the de facto standard for video podcasting.

Podcasting is born

And so with home computers, the Internet, blogging, audio blogging, the MP3 and MP4 formats, and digital media players all coming together in a roundabout way, the wonder that is podcasting was born. Without all these elements coming together in just the right way, podcasting as we know it now might not even exist. The connections among all these diverse technologies could be examined in much deeper detail, but for now, it will suffice to say that podcasting exists. Hooray!

What's in a Name?

Why is podcasting called *podcasting* and not *digital delivery* or *MP3casting*? Well, the emergence of the dominant digital media device has a great deal to do with it. With somewhere around 90 percent of the hard drive–based MP3 player market, Apple's iPods have taken the niche by storm. It's arguable that iPods are a cultural phenomenon and an embodiment of a generation's zeitgeist. With tens of millions of iPods hitting the streets in just a few years of sales (in the fiscal quarter January–March 2006 alone, it was reported that Apple sold 8.8 million iPods), who can argue? For the record, Dannie Gregoire of Louisville, Kentucky, is widely credited with coining the term *podcast*. Who knows—without this gentleman, we might have ended up with a lame moniker such as *Intercasting!*

2

Jumping In

OK, so now you know what a podcast is, where it came from, and what sorts of technologies had to come together to make it possible. What's next? Well, you may be champing at the bit to create your own audio or video podcast, but before I show you the ropes on that, I suggest that you learn a little more about the podcasting universe in general.

This chapter examines the various programs that scour the Internet for podcasts of all kinds, allowing you to get just the right podcasts for you. This section also touches on podcasting content, resources, commercial podcasting, Internet and traditional radio, television and streaming video, and computer and digital music device (MP3 players) podcast players for both audio and video podcasts. By the time you finish this chapter, the art of downloading and enjoying podcasts will be second nature.

When podcasting is mentioned from here on out, please note that video podcasting and audio podcasting are included in my definition of podcasting, so I am referring to both audio and video podcasting unless one type is specifically mentioned.

Getting Started

As mentioned in Chapter 1, podcasts can be found all over the World Wide Web in multiple forms, from audio blogs to daily newspapers (in audio form) to celebrity interviews and video "shows." The majority of podcasts, however, are home-brewed gems put together by everyday people in an effort to educate, entertain, or even offend. This section examines how to get your hands on just the right podcasts for you and helps you decide which software best suits your needs. Although the early days of podcasting featured a slew of programs that more or less did one or two things each, now the main pieces of software are refined multifunctional tools that allow you to manage most every aspect of podcasting in one convenient place.

Podcast aggregators (podcatching software)

The software that goes out and grabs podcasts for you is known as an *aggregator*. An aggregator scours the Web for the exact kind of content (podcasts) you have told it to look for. Many of these programs will go out and get the material at night (or whenever you tell it to), delivering the content to your desktop, iPod, or other MP3 player while you sleep. Because many broadband Internet connections are in an always-on state, aggregator software takes advantage of this situation, grabbing content around the clock.

Aggregators are available for Macintosh computers, Windows PCs, Unix/Linux systems, and handheld devices such as PDAs and SmartPhones.

 Aggregator is the technical term for a piece of software that collects and downloads podcasts, but the more friendly way to refer to it is to use the term *podcatcher*. In this book, *aggregator* and *podcatcher* are used interchangeably.

Many great pieces of software are out there to help you capture podcasts, but for the beginner, I recommend two products. For the Macintosh, I suggest iTunes. For Linux and handheld devices, I suggest iPodder. For Windows, I recommend HappyFish and iPodder (and, of course, iTunes for Windows). Starting out with these programs will ensure a smooth entry into the world of capturing and enjoying podcasts.

BashPodder

Required Software: Xdialog (Mac only)
OS Requirement: Mac OS X, Linux
Price: Freeware

BashPodder (http://linc.homeunix.org:8080/scripts/bashpodder; **Figure 2.1**) is a very simple (only 44 lines of code) aggregator that was designed primarily to work with Linux but works with Mac OS X as well. Basically, all BashPodder does is download MP3 files that are specified in an RSS feed. If you are not familiar with Linux and programming in general, I recommend that you set aside BashPodder, despite its power and simplicity, until you've learned more about tweaking scripts in Linux.

Figure 2.1

BashPodder is a very simple Mac/Linux option for grabbing podcasts.

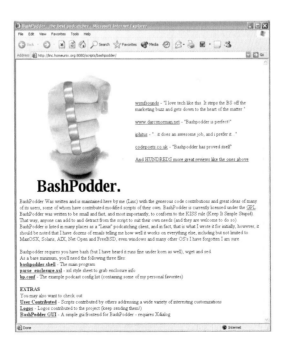

note On the Macintosh, BashPodder requires Xdialog, a program that allows command-line interfaces to appear in dialog boxes rather than just as lines of text in a window.

FeederReader

win
Required Software: Microsoft .NET Framework 1.1, Microsoft ActiveSync
OS Requirement: Windows Mobile
Price: Freeware ($9 donation requested)

FeederReader is a full-featured podcatcher for RSS feeds for the Pocket PC crowd running Windows Mobile. One key difference between many home computers and handheld devices like Pocket PCs is that the latter

Figure 2.2
FeederReader is a full-featured RSS aggregator for those who use Windows Mobile on Pocket PCs and similar devices.

are not always connected to the Internet, which somewhat limits their ability to update podcasts frequently. Despite this limitation, FeederReader (www.feederreader.com; **Figure 2.2**) does an excellent job of managing podcasting feeds for Windows Mobile users.

FeederReader can be configured to update podcasts only when it is connected to the Internet (obviously) and download the content as quickly as possible so that it can be stored for later use from the Pocket PC. Although FeederReader can be used by the beginner podcast enthusiast, its in-depth functionality and ability to show error messages and scripts in detail make it a better choice for the more seasoned podcast listener.

Following are some of FeederReader's features:

- Can be stored directly on a flash memory card

- Can handle a large number of feeds

- Provides detailed error messaging

- Keeps statistics on all loaded files

- Supports OPML (Outline Processor Markup Language) import and export

HappyFish

Required Software: Microsoft .NET Framework 1.1
OS Requirement: Windows 2000 or XP
Price: Freeware

HappyFish, shown in **Figure 2.3**, is the brainchild of Will Corum and Danny Boyd, and was designed as an RSS enclosure aggregator (see the note in this section). HappyFish is a very user-friendly piece of software that works on Windows-based PCs and that can be downloaded from http://thirstycrow.net/happyfish/default.aspx.

Figure 2.3

HappyFish is a solid choice for a Windows PC podcatcher.

An RSS enclosure can be any file from a movie to a picture to news headlines to audio files such as podcasts. When I refer to RSS enclosures, I am speaking of files that are put out on the Internet for anyone to access and download.

I should note, however, that for HappyFish to work properly, you must have Microsoft .NET Framework 1.1 running on your machine. This is a piece of background software that is published by Microsoft and is available from its Web site. The HappyFish Web site also contains a link to the Microsoft .NET Framework 1.1 site for your convenience.

HappyFish is an excellent one-stop podcatcher for a Windows PC, giving the user plenty of flexibility, including the following features:

- The ability to add an unlimited number of feeds

- Control over when and how often feeds are checked for new material

- The ability to have multiple devices updated (with different content) from the same PC

- The ability to catalog content so that you can see what's available and choose what to download rather than downloading everything there, which can save on bandwidth considerably

- An easy-to-use interface

- A built-in Web browser, making it easy to obtain RSS feed addresses without leaving the HappyFish program

iPodder 2.1

Required Software: None (iTunes suggested)
OS Requirement: Mac OS X 10.2.3 or later, Windows 2000 or XP, Linux
Price: Freeware

iPodder (www.ipodder.org; **Figure 2.4**), created by Adam Curry and Dave Winer, is arguably the program that got the whole podcasting ball rolling in the first place. iPodder was the aggregator of choice until Apple added a podcasting feature set to iTunes; even so, iPodder is still a popular and powerful podcatcher.

Figure 2.4
iPodder, the granddaddy of podcatchers, has evolved into an elegant and useful program. The Windows version is shown here.

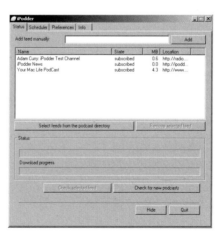

iPodder is a small program designed simply to download audio files from selected podcasts to your computer, an MP3 player, or an iPod, and is packaged in a way that makes it accessible to all users.

The Macintosh version of iPodder, shown in **Figure 2.5**, is more pleasing visually than its Windows counterpart, but underneath the facades, these two siblings function in much the same way.

Figure 2.5

The Macintosh version of iPodder is also a solid performer.

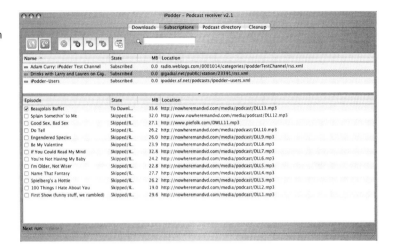

 Current Mac iPodder specifications: If you want to run iPodder, you need to have a Mac that is capable of running Mac OS X 10.3 or later.

iPodder offers the following handy features:

- The ability to feed subscriptions manually or automatically. (Note that iPodder has a default channel that introduces you to several podcasts and podcast directories, instantly giving you access to a world of podcasts.)

- The ability to check for new podcasts manually or to schedule specific times.

- The ability to hide in the background while it completes its searching and downloading functions.

- Automatic downloading of podcasts to your MP3 player.

- Automatic downloading of podcasts to iTunes (Windows or Mac) and your iPod (if that is your player of choice).

iPodder.NET

Required Software: Microsoft .NET Framework 1.1
OS Requirement: Windows 2000 or XP
Price: Freeware

iPodder.NET (http://ipoddernet.sourceforge.net; **Figure 2.6**) is a simple Windows-based aggregator that is very simple and no-frills in nature but nonetheless gets the job done.

Figure 2.6

iPodder.NET is a simple podcatcher for Windows PCs.

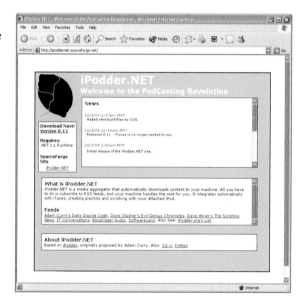

Like HappyFish, iPodder.NET requires that Microsoft .NET Framework 1.1 be installed on your Windows 2000 or Windows XP machine before you can even install it.

In its current incarnation, iPodder.NET is designed to work with iTunes (the PC version, of course), ferrying all downloaded podcasts into the iTunes library, from where they can be transferred to the user's iPod.

Once it's installed and running, iPodder.NET actually functions in the background, and as such, it may appeal to those who don't want to have to open and close a program repeatedly to complete aggregator tasks. iPodder.NET sits in the system tray, which in most Windows configurations is near the date-and-time area. When you right-click

Figure 2.7
The iPodder.NET icon is a small black lemon on a blue background with a pair of iPod headphones on it. Right-click this icon to get at the Configuration panel.

the program's icon in the system tray (**Figure 2.7**) and choose Options from the shortcut menu, the iPodder.NET Configuration panel appears.

This panel is very simple. Cut and paste the feeds you desire into the Add Feed box and then click the Retrieve Now! button to gather up all the podcasts from that feed. In the top-right corner is a spot to set the refresh time for iPodder.NET to check the feeds for new material; you can set this option from 1 minute to 999 minutes.

Once the feeds are in place, there is no need to open the iPodder.NET application and fool with anything. Indeed, the podcasts go directly to iTunes or to a specified folder on the hard drive, and everything happens in the background. To add a new feed, you need only right-click the icon in the system tray to open the iPodder.NET Configuration panel; otherwise, the program runs entirely in the background.

iPodder.NET is not flashy, but it certainly gets the job done, especially for those using Apple's free iTunes software to manage their audio files.

iTunes 6.0.4

Required Software: None
OS Requirement: Mac OS 10.2.8 or later, Windows 2000 or XP
Price: Free

For those using the more than 40 million iPods (this number grows by more than a million every month that passes), Apple's iTunes (www.apple.com/itunes; **Figure 2.8**) is the software they are most

Figure 2.8
The Windows version of iTunes is similar to its Macintosh counterpart.

likely using to manage their digital music and book libraries. The program also provides a portal directly to the iTunes Music Store, allowing users to purchase songs for 99 cents a pop and books for varying prices. In late June 2005, however, Apple announced the release of iTunes 4.9, with a built-in podcast aggregator that gives you access to thousands of free podcasts, ranging from ABC News to Penn Jillette to Al Franken to the hottest podcasts burning up the charts at any given time. Adding a podcast aggregator (podcatcher) to arguably the most complete and functional of the digital audio organizers makes perfect sense, and Apple has risen to the occasion.

What makes iTunes special is that for users of Apple's iPods, it's truly an all-in-one solution. For Macintosh users, iTunes ties in with iPhoto, iMovie, GarageBand, and iWeb, but even as a stand-alone product, iTunes rules the roost. iTunes brings together Internet radio, your library of music, audiobooks, podcasts, video podcasts, the iTunes

Figure 2.9

The Source list in iTunes shows all the various sources of content available to you.

Music Store, and other video content (such as music videos or home movies), all in one easy-to-use place (**Figure 2.9**). It's an impressive collection of interlocking parts that make navigating the digital-media realm a simple exercise.

As of this writing, iTunes is up to version 6.0.4. To access podcasts you already have stored in iTunes, simply click the Podcasts icon directly below the Library icon in the iTunes Source list.

iTunes 6.0.4 also allows you to set the usual parameters, such as how often iTunes checks for new episodes of your favorite podcasts and how many episodes of each podcast to keep, as well as preferences for how these podcasts are transferred (or not) to your iPod(s).

The Macintosh software suite iLife '06—iTunes, GarageBand, iDVD, iMovie, iPhoto, and iWeb—allows for the creation of video and/or audio podcasts as well as the publication of those podcasts. The great part is that iLife '06 is an all-in-one solution that allows the user to create a podcast and get it out there for the world to hear/watch in a matter of minutes. Check out Chapter 5 to see how to publish your podcast using iWeb.

jPodder

Required Software: Java version 1.4 or later
OS Requirement: Windows 98, 2000, or XP; Linux
Price: Freeware

One of the early entries in the aggregator software derby, jPodder (www.jpodder.com; **Figure 2.10**) is a solid candidate with a very full set of features. Installing jPodder can be a bit of a headache, however, because it requires that you have Java version 1.4 or later. That said, the software bundle contains all the information you need to install all the requisite software and program files to get yourself up and running on your Linux box or Windows PC.

Figure 2.10

jPodder is a capable and useful podcatcher for the Linux and Windows crowds.

jPodder has a very complete feature set, including the ability to incorporate detailed information (such as images, artist information, and bit-rate data) about each podcast or file. Here is the feature set for jPodder:

- Because it is Java-based, jPodder can be installed on multiple systems.

- jPodder has a built-in user manual.

- On a Windows PC, jPodder can sit in the system tray (like iPodder.NET) to work in the background.

- Subscription feeds can be given detailed information.

- The program has drag-and-drop functionality.

- jPodder includes a built-in media player.

- The program supports transfers to iTunes and WMP (Windows Media Player).

Nimiq

win

Required Software: Microsoft .NET Framework 1.1 or later
OS Requirement: Windows 2000 or XP
Price: Donation

Nimiq (www.nimiq.nl) is another solid podcast aggregator for the Windows PCs of the world. Like many of the other PC aggregators, Nimiq requires that Microsoft .NET Framework 1.1 or later be installed on your machine before you can install and run it. That said, installing Nimiq and getting the podcasting ball rolling are a breeze, although the feature set is somewhat limited compared with those of its contemporaries.

Nimiq has two main sections: the main screen, where subscriptions and enclosures can be viewed and accessed (**Figure 2.11**), and the OPML Browser.

Figure 2.11

Nimiq is very basic, but it's easy to use and very stable.

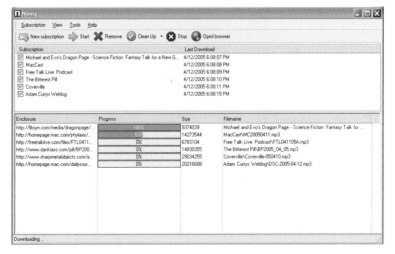

OPML stands for *Outline Processor Markup Language,* a format for outlines. (An outline refers to the structure of the file, which looks something like an outline with various layers.) Outlines using OPML are very flexible and are well suited for RSS feeds. Nimiq's OPML Browser allows users to navigate many RSS feeds and then subscribe to those feeds or download them from directly inside the browser.

Nimiq has the ability to import and export files, and it has a History area where the podcast file transactions are logged. To set up schedules for checking RSS feeds, you use the Options panel (**Figure 2.12**),

Figure 2.12

Despite its simplicity, Nimiq has plenty of useful features.

which you access from the Tools menu. Like other aggregators of this sort, Nimiq lets you choose where file downloads are saved, how often Nimiq should check for new files to download, and how long to keep the downloaded podcasts.

Nimiq doesn't interact directly with iTunes, and it doesn't have a media player built in; however, it is more than capable of playing your

Microsoft .NET Framework 1.1

Microsoft's .NET Framework is a *development environment* (a set of tools that allows programmers to develop software) that allows different programming languages to work together to improve the way in which Windows-based software works for the end user. The .NET Framework is a collection of five kinds of development tools: Web services, client-to-server, service-to-service, server-to-server, and client-to-client tools.

Entire books have been written about the .NET Framework, but for the purposes of this book, you simply need to know that this Windows tool helps such disparate devices and concepts as cell phones and podcasts come together through software running on a Windows-based PC. The result is fantastic pieces of software (like the ones I'm examining here) that improve your interaction and experiences with the Internet and World Wide Web, as well as with any electronic devices you may connect to them.

podcasts through Windows Media Player. You need not use WMP to play the podcasts; indeed, you can simply save the podcast files to a specific directory and then move them manually to an MP3 player whenever necessary.

In summary, Nimiq is a fine podcast aggregator, but if you are using an iPod and iTunes, it will behoove you to look at other programs, such as iPodder 2.1 and HappyFish.

Now Playing

win   video

Required Software: iTunes or Windows Media Player
OS Requirement: Windows 2000 or XP
Price: Freeware

Designed by Brandon Fuller, Now Playing (http://brandon.fuller.name/archives/hacks/nowplaying; **Figure 2.13**) is a podcast aggregator that is distinctly different from the others in that it is not a stand-alone program, but a plug-in for Windows Media Player or an iTunes PC. A *plug-in* is an add-on program that requires the presence of another program to function. Plug-ins are usually designed specifically to add features or functionality to a particular program, and Now Playing is no exception to this rule.

Figure 2.13

As a plug-in rather than a stand-alone program, Now Playing isn't fancy, but it gets the job done.

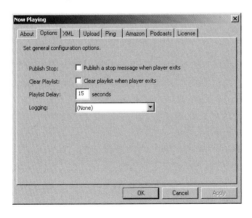

> **tip**
>
> One excellent feature of Now Playing is that it also acts as a podcast server, getting podcasts (or other audio files) you've made out to the kind folks on the Internet.

Because Now Playing is an iTunes plug-in, any podcasts that are downloaded are placed directly in iTunes and then on your iPod. Entering feeds in Now Playing is a breeze. When you start iTunes after installing Now Playing, a prompt shows up with a panel that allows you to enter the feeds for your favorite podcasts and to set the parameters for checking those feeds.

A unique feature of Now Playing is the Amazon tab, which allows you to connect with one of Amazon.com's Web sites to coordinate album art and other data.

Because Apple's iPod has swept through the world and has become the dominant digital music device, many users rely on iTunes to manage their MP3 collections. Still, there are many who have not joined the iPod generation, and for those folks, Now Playing also exists as a plug-in for Windows Media Player.

PlayPod

Required Software: None
OS Requirement: Mac OS X
Price: Free trial; then $16.99

Designed specifically for Mac OS X, PlayPod is a very slick, powerful podcatcher and news reader that is an excellent choice for newbies and experts alike.

One of the most impressive features of PlayPod is its built-in tutorial, Getting Started with PlayPod (www.iggsoftware.com/playpod. This mini-tutorial covers the main bases of podcasting's background and function, making it easy for first-time users to get a handle on the key concepts involved in this new medium.

PlayPod comes with an easy-to-use master window that includes three main windows: a general directory window, a directory file window, and a media player window that functions as both a media player and a source of information for the individual podcast that has been selected. **Figure 2.14** shows the PlayPod master window in action.

Figure 2.14

Like other polished podcatchers, PlayPod is as easy on the eyes as it is to operate and enjoy.

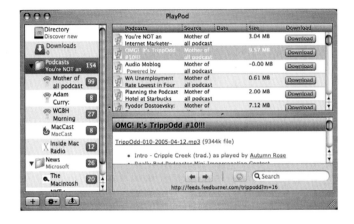

PocketRSS

Required Software: None

OS Requirement: Windows Mobile

Price: Free trial; then $5.95

PocketRSS (**Figure 2.15**) is an aggregator for Pocket PCs that was designed by HappyJackRoad (www.happyjackroad.net), a company

Figure 2.15

PocketRSS is a solid choice for Pocket PC users who want access to advanced options in a podcatcher.

that has been around since 2001. PocketRSS (up to version 2.1.6 at this writing) is a Today Screen plug-in and stand-alone application that allows the movement of podcasts and other RSS data to the Today Screen. (Those with Pocket PCs will know what that means.)

A solid aggregator for Pocket PC users, PocketRSS offers the following features:

- Simple RSS feed content management

- Namespace/XML mapping features for advanced users

- Full feed item control

- Ability to download when connected to Internet and store for offline viewing/listening at a later date

PoddumFeeder

Required Software: None
OS Requirement: Mac OS X 10.3
Price: $4.95

> **note**
>
> The $4.95 is a suggested donation to If Then software. If you do not donate this small amount of money, you are limited to subscribing to three podcasts.

PoddumFeeder (www.ifthensoft.com; **Figure 2.16**) is a straight-up, Macintosh-only podcast aggregator. It is very simple to install and use, and has most of the features we have come to expect from quality software.

Figure 2.16

PoddumFeeder is a quality Macintosh aggregator.

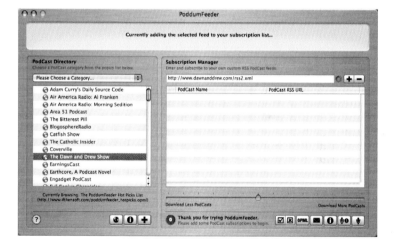

As a bonus, PoddumFeeder has a couple of unique features that allow it to stand out from the crowd a little. The first of these features allows you to e-mail a podcast. When you click the Email a Podcast URL button, you can send podcast feed URLs directly to your friends without having to leave the cozy confines of PoddumFeeder's interface. The other handy feature is a long slider bar labeled Download Less Podcasts at one end and Download More Podcasts at the other end. By moving this slider, you can adjust the number of podcasts that will be downloaded from each particular feed. Although not particularly concrete, it's an easy-to-use, enjoyable feature.

Pod2Go

Required Software: None

OS Requirement: Mac OS X 10.2.7 or later

Price: Free with registration

Pod2Go (www.kainjow.com/pod2go) is a podcast aggregator, but it's also much more. Pod2Go includes feeds for a wide range of other handy information that is available on the World Wide Web through RSS. In fact, when you first run Pod2Go, there will likely be a moment of shock when you see all the things it can do. The list includes

- News

- Weather

- Movie times

- Stocks

- Horoscopes

- Lyrics

- Text

- Driving directions (**Figure 2.17**)

- Applications

- Backups

- Podcasts

- Launcher, a built-in utility that makes it easy to open applications and documents from inside Pod2Go

Figure 2.17

Talk about versatility! Among other things, Pod2Go offers driving directions.

Pod2Go is truly an amazing piece of software, with everything you need built right in. In fact, the only thing you really need to make Pod2Go sing is a broadband Internet connection.

Many people have speculated about where podcasting will go in the future, and although that is open for debate, the future of podcast aggregators is here with Pod2Go, because there is just so much available information funneling through one place. If getting information other than podcasts turns you off, I recommend that you steer clear of Pod2Go. But if you want to have access to the maximum amount of data and services, this piece of software is worth a closer look.

RSSRadio

win

Required Software: .NET Framework 1.1
OS Requirement: Windows 2000 or XP
Price: $4.95

RSSRadio (www.dorada.co.uk; **Figure 2.18**) is rated in Podcast Alley's software area as one of the best podcatchers, and it's obvious why.

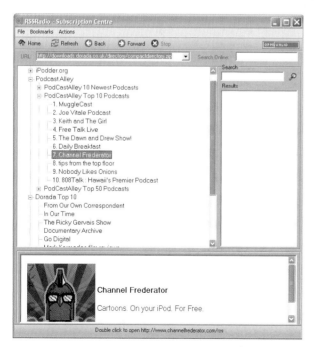

RSSRadio has an easy-to-use graphical interface; it integrates with iTunes, WMP, and the jRiver Media Center; and it includes features like an automatic right-click subscription from Internet Explorer or Firefox (which means that you can subscribe to podcasts from inside your Web browser).

Figure 2.18

A highly rated podcatcher, RSSRadio is an excellent choice for the Windows PC crowd.

Some of its other features are

- Advanced plug-in object model that allows expansion of RSSRadio's functionality

- Advanced iPod features

- Resumption of interrupted downloads where they left off

- Audio Player previews of podcasts without downloading them

- Embedded Web browser

- Capability to serve as a standard RSS/ATOM newsreader

Transistr

Required Software: iTunes 4 or later
OS Requirement: Mac OS X 10.3.5 or later
Price: Free trial; then $19.95

Designed by August Trometer and Ray Slakinski, Transistr (http://transistr.com; **Figure 2.19**), formerly known as iPodderX, is a Macintosh-only aggregator that goes further than iPodder 2.1 in terms of functionality. Transistr allows the user to download audio files, and because it is fully integrated with iTunes, the program makes it easy for Mac users to manage their podcasts.

Figure 2.19

Transistr is a good choice for the Macintosh if iTunes isn't your cup of tea.

Transistr also manages images, and because it takes advantage of Apple's iPhoto software, it makes managing visual content easy. Finally, Transistr can go out and grab video footage that you can view with the program's built-in media player (**Figure 2.20**).

Figure 2.20

When video media is selected, a flap slides out from the side of the Transistr window to allow viewing of the content in the built-in media player.

Transistr is an excellent choice for anyone who wants to stand ready on the frontiers of podcasting. The program contains a Special Directory of podcasts that is continuously updated. At this writing, the directory has more than 16,000 podcasts in it, which should be enough to get even the most voracious podcast listener started.

With its built-in media player and its ability to grab virtually any kind of file attached to an RSS feed, Transistr is a fantastic catch-all program that will likely take care of the immediate podcasting needs of even the most hard-core users.

Some of the features and advantages of Transistr are

- The ability to manage audio files, images, video files, and virtually any kind of file attached to an RSS feed

- The ability to deliver content right to your Mac and ultimately to iTunes and your iPod or iPod photo

- Slick, easy-to-use interface

- Easy installation

- Built-in Special Directory with thousands of podcasts to choose among

Interview with Transistr Creator August Trometer

*In the first edition of this book, the software was called iPodderX. That has since changed, and the software is now called Transistr. I caught up with **August Trometer** again to find out what's happened in the year since the first book was released.*

Farkas: Why did iPodderX change its name to Transistr?

Trometer: Apple is very protective of the iPod name and brand. Unfortunately, they felt that the name iPodderX was an infringement. This, though, was a good thing for us. We always felt that podcasting was much bigger than just iPods, and the iPodderX name sort of locked us into that. We're very happy with the new name—Transistr—and we have a lot of great plans for the product.

Farkas: What has surprised you the most in the past 6 months when it comes to podcasting?

Trometer: I think the tremendous growth is what has surprised me the most. When I first became involved with podcasting, it wasn't even called that! There were probably a hundred or so people in the world who knew what it was. Since then, the interest has exploded. When corporate America gets involved, you know that the idea has taken root, and so many big corporations are using podcasting as a part of their business. It's stunning, really, especially since I know what it was like when the concept was born.

Farkas: Where do you see video podcasting going in the future?

Trometer: The cliché used to be that everyone who wanted one was going have their own TV channel. I think podcasting, especially video podcasting, is the way this is going to happen. The tools to make your own show are now widely available and inexpensive. All it takes is a good idea and a little time.

Plus if you take a look at the 2004 elections, bloggers were a primary force in changing the outcome. Now imagine those same bloggers with microphones and video cameras. Big media is going to lose its hold, and fresh, new voices are going to take its place.

Farkas: What predictions do you have about podcasting in the coming year?

Trometer: I think we've only seen the beginning for podcasting. While it may be growing in mindshare, only a small percentage of people actually make use of podcasts on a daily basis. I think you'll see that number climb dramatically. You'll also see more people getting involved on the content-creation side. As the tools become more available and easier to use, more people will want to share their voices with the world.

TVTonic

Required Software: None
OS Requirement: Windows 2000 or XP
Price: Free

TVTonic (www.tvtonic.com) is one of the most exciting new podcatchers to hit the market. Two very interesting features set it apart from the other podcatchers. First, TVTonic is used exclusively for video podcasting content. The second interesting feature is that TVTonic is Web-based, taking place entirely in your Web browser (**Figure 2.21**).

Figure 2.21

TVTonic is accessed entirely from the Web.

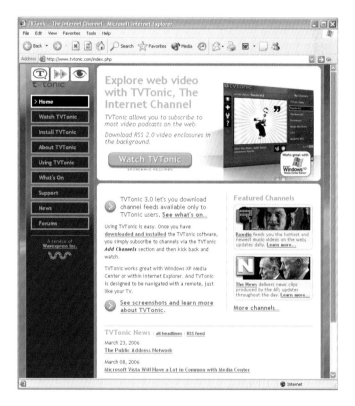

With TVTonic, you can subscribe to (**Figure 2.22**), manage, and watch video podcasts all in one place: your Web browser. Video content is downloaded in the background, making the experience seamless. Both WMP and QuickTime are supported by TVTonic, making it easy to install and use on a wide range of PC systems. Although you can access any of the thousands of video podcasts available with TVTonic, it also gives you access to MoviePick, which is a channel dedicated exclusively to movie trailers, and to several other exclusive channels, including news, animated shorts, cartoons, and music videos. TVTonic is one of the most exciting new products in the video podcasting realm.

Figure 2.22
TV Tonic offers several video channels outside the podcasting realm.

Setting up TVTonic is a breeze. Simply go to www.tvtonic.com and click the Install TVTonic button; that's it. After the program is installed, you are taken to a Web page where you can choose which channels you'd like to subscribe to. It's an exciting new access point for video podcasts and Internet video content in general.

TVTonic is easy to use and works on nearly any contemporary Windows-based computer, but it does require a broadband connection to the Internet. If you don't have broadband, TVTonic is out of reach.

Starting with iTunes on the Mac or PC

Start by going to Apple's iTunes Web site at www.apple.com/itunes. From the download page, you can select which version of iTunes to download (Windows or Mac). When the software is downloaded, click the installer to install iTunes on your computer, it's as easy as that!

When iTunes is installed, you can use it as a home base for all your digital music, audiobooks, home movies, and music videos, and even for Internet radio tuning (**Figure 2.23**).

Figure 2.23

iTunes is a full-featured product, to say the least. Shown here is the Internet radio service.

That said, the reason you want iTunes right now is for the podcasts, so click Podcasts in the Source list on the left side of the screen. When you're in the Podcasts area, you should see an empty list. In the bottom-left corner, however, is a button that says Podcast Directory; click that.

When you're in the Podcast Directory (which is actually part of the iTunes Music Store, as shown in **Figure 2.24**), you can access podcasts in several ways, including:

- Clicking Movie Trailers or Music Videos (for video podcasting aficionados)

- Checking podcasts in the New & Notable section

- Clicking categories ranging from Arts & Entertainment to Science and Public Radio

- Searching for podcasts via a keyword

- Choosing items from the Top 100 Podcasts lists

Figure 2.24

The Podcast Directory in the iTunes Music Store.

Apple's podcasting area also includes 12 colorful buttons, each representing a major category of podcasts; clicking any of these buttons narrows your search to that category. Perhaps the most powerful tool is the Search tool, which allows you to search for podcasts simply by entering one or more keywords. A search of the words *Star Trek*, for example, quickly produced a list of 68 "Star Trek"–related podcasts. Note that to subscribe to any of these podcasts, you need only click the Subscribe button next to that specific podcast title.

When you have found the podcasts you desire, and the subscriptions are in place, you can go into the iTunes Preferences window to fine-tune your podcasting experience. The Preferences windows look very different on a Mac and on a Windows PC (**Figure 2.25** and **Figure 2.26**, respectively), but they contain the same functionality.

Figure 2.25
The Macintosh iTunes Preferences window.

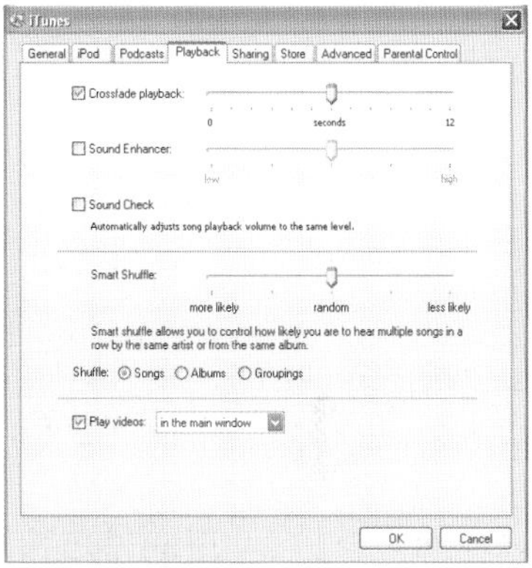

Figure 2.26
The Windows iTunes Preferences window.

Starting with iPodder on the Mac

After you have downloaded iPodder onto your Mac, click the iPodder icon (it looks like a fresh lemon), and the program will be installed on your Mac. When you run iPodder, you will be connected with a couple of welcome messages, including one from Adam Curry himself. To get started with iPodder, you can click the Subscriptions button and then click the Add a New Feed button to enter your own RSS feed address, as shown in **Figure 2.27**.

Figure 2.27
Add a new feed.

Figure 2.28

Podcast feeds from Podcast Alley look like this.

As mentioned earlier in this chapter, Podcast Alley (www.podcastalley.com) is an excellent place to find a podcasting feed. Just click the Subscribe to Podcast link of the podcast that interests you to see the address. **Figure 2.28** shows an example of a subscription address that has been pulled up on Podcast Alley's Web site. After you have a feed URL cut and pasted (or typed) into the window, click the Save button to save the feed in the iPodder library.

Next, you can check for new content by clicking the Check for New Podcasts button (the green button with two arrows on it), and iPodder will do the rest. It will find the new podcasts; download them to your machine; and place them in iTunes, which will ultimately place the podcasts on your iPod the next time you connect it to your Mac to update its contents.

There are five separate iPodder tabs, and each has a distinct function.

The Downloads tab contains up-to-the-second information about just what is being downloaded and from where (**Figure 2.29**), whereas the Podcast Directory tab contains a series of folders with various headings, each of which contains a list of pertinent podcasts. You can add podcasts to the directory simply by clicking the Add button after you've entered the podcast feed URL. Not surprisingly, you can also add or remove folders and subdirectories as you see fit.

Figure 2.29

This window contains download information.

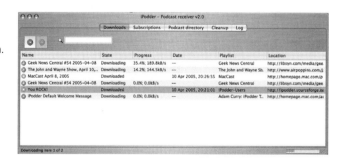

The Subscriptions tab shows you at a glance exactly what podcasts you have subscribed to and which podcasts are already being checked for new material.

The Cleanup tab is for managing files specific to each podcasting feed that you are subscribed to. This allows you to see what files are taking up space on your hard drive so that you can decide whether to keep them or turf them.

The last tab is the Log tab, which quite simply logs every action undertaken by the iPodder software. If you want to check to see whether a particular podcast downloaded successfully, for example, a quick look at the Log tab will answer your query.

Starting with HappyFish on the PC

To begin with, ensure that your machine has Microsoft .NET Framework 1.1; then you can install HappyFish. After Microsoft .NET Framework 1.1 is installed and you have downloaded HappyFish, you can run the installer to place it on your machine. Start it up, and you'll see the basic program front end, shown in **Figure 2.30**. Then, by choosing Feed > Add Feed, you can add any RSS feed your heart desires. RSS feeds look just like the URLs you've come to know.

Figure 2.30
HappyFish is a great place to start on a Windows PC if iTunes isn't your thing.

There are several fantastic reservoirs of RSS feeds, not the least of which is Podcast Alley. Find the podcasting feed that you want to use by clicking the Subscribe to Podcast link (on Podcast Alley's Web site; it may be different on other sites). To attach a feed to HappyFish (or any similar aggregator), just cut and paste the feed's URL into the Add Feed window, and voilà! As soon as you complete this task, HappyFish goes out and gets the files available from that feed, as shown in **Figure 2.31**.

Figure 2.31

Add a new podcast feed.

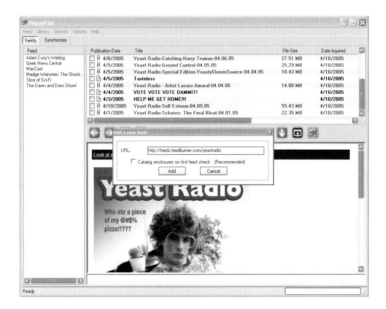

Next up, you can adjust how often the HappyFish software goes out and checks for new files on each feed. After you choose Feed > Global Application Settings, a window pops up, allowing you to select how often and when you want HappyFish to go looking for content (Global Feed Check Settings). After all your feeds are set up, you need only let HappyFish do the work while you sit back and enjoy the podcasts it brings to your electronic doorstep.

Now that you've got HappyFish downloading all the great podcasts you want to listen to, you may want to set the program up to download the podcasts automatically to your digital music player, such as an iPod or any other MP3 player. When you choose Devices > Add Device or Devices > Device Management, you can configure as many digital music player devices as you want to designate as destinations where HappyFish places downloaded podcasts.

Comparing podcatchers

Table 2.1 compares all the podcatchers presented in this chapter. With this table, you can establish the best aggregators for you at a glance and disregard programs that you cannot run due to the computer or OS you use.

Table 2.1: Podcatchers (Podcast Aggregators)

Program	OS	Extra Software Needed?	Stand-Alone Program?	Built-In Media Player?
BashPodder	Mac OS X, Linux	Yes	Yes	No
FeederReader	Windows Mobile	Yes	Yes	No
HappyFish	Windows	Yes	Yes	Yes
iPodder 2.1	Windows, Mac, Linux	No	Yes	Yes
iPodder.NET	Windows	Yes	Yes	Yes
iTunes 6.0.4	Mac OS X, Windows	No	Yes	Yes
jPodder	Windows, Linux	Yes	Yes	Yes
Nimiq	Windows	Yes	Yes	No
Now Playing	Windows	Yes	No	No
PlayPod	Mac	No	Yes	Yes
PocketRSS	Windows Mobile	Yes	Yes	No
PoddumFeeder	Mac	No	Yes	Yes
Pod2Go	Mac	No	Yes	Yes
RSSRadio	Windows	Yes	Yes	No
Transistr	Mac	Yes	Yes	Yes
TVTonic	Windows	No*	No	Yes

*TVTonic uses your Web browser as its front end, so although it technically does require software (a Web browser), the ubiquitous nature of Web browsers like Internet Explorer makes the point moot.

Podscope: Google for Podcasts

During the writing of the first edition of this book, a very cool technology emerged for helping folks find the exact podcasts they want to find. You don't need a podcatcher to get this material; indeed, you need only a connection to the Internet and a World Wide Web browser to take advantage of this powerful tool. Podscope (www.podscope.com) allows you to search the vast (and growing) library of podcasts for specific words or phrases; then it displays the results (**Figure 2.32**), complete with audio clips from each podcast that contains the phrase you're looking for!

Podscope is a one-stop search engine that is (currently) exclusively for podcasts. Developed by a company called TVEyes, Podscope uses proprietary technology to listen to each podcast and then convert that information to text strings that can be searched. Currently, Podscope is available on the World Wide Web and is an amazing technology that is already the best nonpodcatcher way to find podcasting content of all sorts. The power of tools like Podscope can actually change the shape of the medium itself. By being able to sift through tens of thousands of podcasts quickly and easily to find mention of a specific or rare disease, for example, the listener can save many hours of searching and perhaps hear something he would have missed otherwise.

Figure 2.32

When you search for a phrase or a word in Podscope, a list of all the podcasts containing that phrase or word quickly appears onscreen, including short audio clips that include the spoken portions of the phrase you are looking for.

Finding Commercial Podcasts

OK, so you have used your podcatcher software to scour the "airwaves" of cyberspace for the content that tickles your fancy the most. But the world of so-called free podcasts is just one portion of the equation. Although some people would disagree, I'm inclined to fit audiobooks into the podcast category, as well as periodicals that are routinely converted to audio format. As mentioned in Chapter 1, Audible.com is one of the forerunners of commercial podcasting, but if you look hard enough (and often, you don't have to look very hard), you can find commercial podcasts all over the place.

Following are locations where you can purchase podcasts and audio-book materials online.

Audible.com

www.audible.com

Around since the late 1990s, Audible.com (**Figure 2.33**) is the dominant audiobook and commercial-podcast-content vendor on the World Wide Web. Audible's principal role is to supply audiobooks in MP3 format for users to listen to on their favorite MP3 players, iPods, or desktop media

players. Voted one of the best sites on the Web in 2003 by CNET.com, Audible has well over 30,000 hours' worth of content for you to explore. Although most of this content has a cost associated with it, Audible offers various subscriptions that lower the effective cost of an audiobook to less than $10.

Certainly, some people would argue that commercial audiobooks are not truly podcasts, but I maintain that any audio program that can be easily downloaded and

Figure 2.33
Audible.com is a great source for commercial podcasts.

enjoyed on a digital music player such as the iPod should be considered in the same breath with so-called free podcasts. The number of available audiobooks has skyrocketed, and because the majority of them are now unabridged and often read by the author, it's hard to argue that the original content (or intent) of a book is lost in the conversion to the aural format. In fact, even though I'm an avid podcast enthusiast, I have more than 150 audiobooks on my 40 GB iPod.

Figure 2.34
Robin Williams's show is exclusive to Audible.com and is absolutely hilarious. The show has a different celebrity guest every week.

The periodicals and subscription shows better fit the traditional podcast mold, however. Indeed, the amount of podcastlike content on Audible.com has expanded greatly in the past couple of years; it now includes audio versions of popular newspapers, magazines, and radio shows, and even custom-made podcasts such as the fantastically funny "RobinWilliams@Audible.com" show (**Figure 2.34**).

For Free or Not for Free: That Is the Question

In the case of some podcast content, it's important to be absolutely sure that you don't have to pay for something before you pay for it. Although that may sound convoluted, there are instances in which podcasts are both available for free and are for sale simultaneously (both legally). The great NPR show "Science Friday," for example, can be bought as a 12-month subscription (the show airs every Friday) for $44.95. A little (very little) digging, however, gets you the exact same content for free via podcasts in the iTunes (or any other) podcast directory. I've come across several of these rather odd contradictions in the past year, so the message is that it's worth checking to make absolutely sure that something isn't available for free (legally).

It's also worth pointing out that some content might be available for free, but it might very well be illegal, so be sure you're doing the right thing before you snap up a "free" program. In the case of "Science Friday," the free podcast is available directly from the show's very own Web site, so it's obviously legal and sanctioned by both NPR and "Science Friday."

Audio Book Club

www.audiobookclub.com

Audio Book Club (**Figure 2.35**) is an online book club that specializes in audiobooks of all kinds, including downloadable podcast-type books. The idea is that you can get just-released audiobooks for a discount of 10 percent to 20 percent by shopping at the club's Web site. Although you can order cassette or CD-based audiobooks, the Audio Book Club also offers downloadable books so that you can have them immediately available on your digital media device or computer.

Figure 2.35
Audio Book Club is another option for online audiobooks.

Audiobooks Online

www.audiobooksonline.com

Audiobooks Online (**Figure 2.36**) is an online merchant that sells (at this time) audiobooks only. The company claims that it will be offering audiobooks in MP3 format for download in the near future, but the one intriguing product it does sell is MP3 CDs of classic books. These files cannot be downloaded—indeed, you must have the CDs shipped to a real mailbox—but they're available for a bevy of classic titles, from Jules Verne's *20,000 Leagues Under the Sea* to Leo Tolstoy's *Anna Karenina*.

Figure 2.36

Audiobooks Online is a source for classic audiobooks.

Blackstone Audiobooks

www.blackstoneaudio.com

Another of the audiobook Web sites, Blackstone Audiobooks (**Figure 2.37**) is unique in that it is an actual producer of audiobook content. You'll find a fair amount of crossover between what is available on Audible.com and what's on BlackstoneAudio.com. Still, this is another good source for audiobooks that are available for immediate download to your digital media player.

Figure 2.37

Many newly released audiobooks are published by Blackstone Audiobooks.

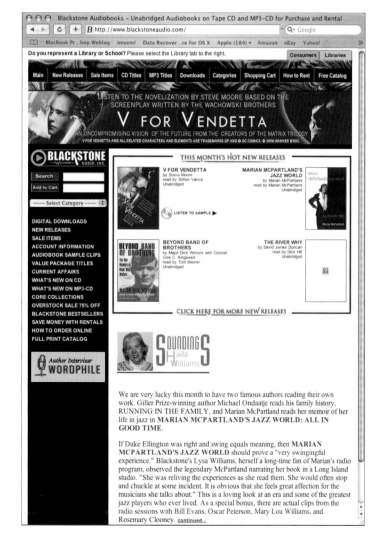

iTunes Music Store

www.apple.com/itunes

Apple's iTunes Music Store (**Figure 2.38**) opened on April 28, 2003, and in slightly more than 3 years since it opened, more than a billion songs (yes, you read that correctly) have been downloaded. The store itself is now available in 15 countries, and by the time you read this book, that number will likely have grown.

Figure 2.38

The iTunes Canada Music Store. Already, more than 1 billion (yes, a 1 with nine 0s after it) music downloads have occurred, and the amount of podcast material in the store is always increasing.

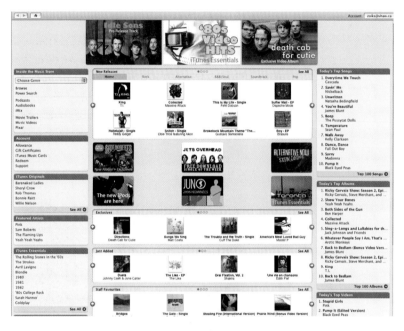

Why does this matter to podcast enthusiasts? As the iTunes Music Store has evolved, an increasing number of podcast-type downloads (other than those available for free in the podcast section) has become available for purchase and download. The kind of content available includes comedy shows, podcasts, and even television talk shows. With the addition of video podcasting to the equation, more video-based products—such as music videos, television shows, and animated shorts—are being sold as well. Although the iTunes Music Store doesn't have quite the selection that Audible.com does, I suspect that this groundbreaking Web site will continue to add podcast content as the phenomenon continues to grow.

Satellite radio

www.xmsatelliteradio.com and www.siriusradio.com

Satellite radio is a novel approach to broadcasting radio. The idea is that a satellite receiver in a home or car provides access to potentially hundreds of radio stations, in categories ranging from classical to children's programming to up-to-date traffic reports around the clock! This service has caught on and now boasts more than 3 million subscribers. Currently, two satellite radio providers are available: XM Satellite Radio and Sirius Satellite Radio.

Like any radio service, however, satellite radio is broadcast live at particular times, making it entirely possible for busy professionals to miss the programming they desire. Not to worry—both XM and Sirius supply streaming podcasts of most of their key shows (**Figure 2.39**), but this is not a free service. If you are already a satellite-radio subscriber, however, the service is included in your fees.

Figure 2.39
XM Satellite Radio is one of two services available in the United States.

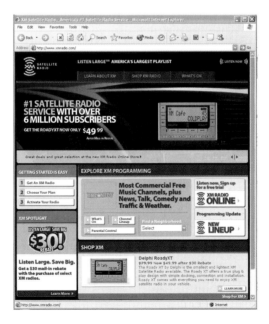

Finding Free Commercial Podcasts

It has been said that the best things in life are free, and when one looks at the vast array of commercial radio shows and other content available as podcasts at no cost, the old saying may just be true after all.

As the phenomenon of podcasting continues to take hold in the general population, there is increasing pressure for producers to make their shows available online so that they can stay connected to their core audience. Indeed, doing so may even help expand their audience. At any rate, publishing shows as podcasts on their Web sites won't hurt their ratings!

AudioBooksForFree.com

www.audiobooksforfree.com

AudioBooksForFree.com (**Figure 2.40**) is a place where you can grab audiobooks in MP3 format for absolutely no cost. How is this possible? The answer lies in the fact that all the books available on this Web site have expired copyrights. Before you become despondent with disappointment, remember that many fantastic classic pieces of fiction can be had for no cost at all, including works by Mark Twain and Edgar Allan Poe, and AudioBooksForFree.com is an excellent resource.

The catch with this Web site is that the quality of the free books is not exactly what you would be willing to pay for. In other words, there is a reason why it is free. The free books sound like they are coming out of a telephone, but for a small charge of between $3 and $6, you can get high-quality versions of the same books. Either way, it's worthwhile to see whether the "free" audio quality is bearable enough for you to enjoy.

Figure 2.40

An audiobook source with a catch: If you want the high-quality version of the audiobooks, you must pay.

Canadian Broadcasting Corporation (CBC)

www.cbc.ca

The Canadian Broadcasting Corporation (CBC) has jumped on the podcasting bandwagon, offering podcasts of several of its radio programs, not the least of which are Tod Maffin's "/Nerd" show and "Quirks & Quarks," hosted by Bob McDonald (**Figure 2.41**).

Figure 2.41

"Quirks & Quarks" was one of the first programs that the CBC podcasted.

The CBC is a large radio and television network that arguably is the glue that holds the large country of Canada together. Like NPR, the CBC is publicly funded, and as such, the podcasts are available for no cost. The up side to the CBC's adoption of this technology is that Canadians living around the world can keep up on happenings in their home country.

Interview with Tod Maffin

Tod Maffin is an international authority on the future of technology in business and media. He speaks to more than 30 conferences around the world each year. Today, he is the national technology columnist for CBC Television's "Canada Now," as well as a national CBC radio host and producer. I caught up with him in Vancouver.

Farkas: Was the idea of podcasting your show on CBC a hard sell?

Maffin: The mandate of CBC is to reflect Canada to Canadians, so we want to do as much as we can do of that, and if podcasting is emerging as a trend, then it behooves us to embrace it. There is cost involved with podcasting, so we're still trying to figure out a cost-effective balance, but since I was already working on a technology column, it made sense to podcast it.

Farkas: How do you think podcasting has expanded your show's audience? Has it?

Maffin: I think it has the potential to expand to a different demographic. Usually, public radio tends to be strong in the upper age demographic. For example, CBC historically is stronger in the 40-plus age range than they are in the under-40 age range, and podcasting helps to open up an entirely new demographic. I think the young people think of public radio as their parents' radio, but if we can deliver it in a medium that they are used to, we can reach them in ways we couldn't before. It is potentially a great way to introduce a younger audience to really intelligent discourse, and secondly, I think it's a way to extend the brand of the public broadcaster.

Farkas: Where do you see podcasting taking the medium of public radio? What effect do you see it having?

Maffin: I think it definitely will have an effect. There are a number of places right now, such as Virgin Radio in the UK, where they strip out all of the music and commercials of a 4-hour morning show and podcast just the DJs talking. The result is like a well-produced 45-minute comedy show. If you can take that stripped-down 40- to 45-minute show and present it as what is essentially a marketing endeavor, then I think it's an incredible opportunity for private radio.

Currently, I am consulting with Australia's public broadcasting service, and they have incredible content that's absolutely perfect for podcasting. It's amazing, the kind of content that's out there and how well it fits into the podcasting paradigm. Public radio has 4-minute documentaries, 12-minute packs; their programming is incredible material for podcasting.

Interview with Tod Maffin *(continued)*

Farkas: Do you envision radio moving toward having everything available in podcast format?

Maffin: Absolutely. Why should broadcasters spend money on terrestrial transmitters and regulation from their country's broadcast regulator when they can produce content and distribute it electronically? Every public radio broadcaster from the BBC to the CBC is governed by an act of parliament or government, so they must by definition broadcast in terrestrial radio, but that doesn't mean that they can't offer value-added services in the form of podcasts. Imagine if we could take an award-winning documentary in one country and make it available via podcast to the entire world. This technology will allow the dissemination of fantastic content into countries and across borders in ways that were previously not possible.

Internet radio

Internet radio (shown in Windows Media Player in **Figure 2.42**) is a form of streaming audio in which traditional radio stations broadcast on the Internet for anyone to listen. With hundreds of stations from all over the planet, Internet radio can make for some very interesting listening sessions. Want to listen to a pop radio station in London or hear about traffic in Moscow? Internet radio is the medium for you!

Figure 2.42

Internet radio opens the entire world to your ears. As long as you have a connection to the 'net, you're in.

Some would argue that Internet radio is also a form of podcasting, but because Internet radio involves live streaming audio, it is not podcasting per se. That said, there are software packages available, such as Replay Radio (www.replay-radio.com), that allow you to record any Internet radio show and then turn it into an MP3 file for download to your iPod or other digital music device. At $29.95, the software isn't inexpensive, but if you are a big fan of the programming available on Internet radio, it will be money well spent.

The Stars Embrace Podcasting

Increasingly, celebrities are joining the ranks of podcasters by putting their content out on the Web for all to hear (for free). Celebrities who are already actively podcasting include Bill Maher, Penn Jillette (**Figure 2.43**), Ricky Gervais, and Garrison Keillor, and even shows like "The Man Show" are offering up podcasts. Although podcasts of this nature usually are fairly short, these podcasts are often extremely entertaining and well worth the price (nothing) of admission!

Figure 2.43

Penn Jillette (the speaking half of Penn and Teller) has his own podcast available for free.

KYOU Radio (and radio stations everywhere)

www.kyouradio.com

KYOU Radio (**Figure 2.44**), a radio station in the Bay Area of California, was the first station to go to an all-podcast format. KYOU is unique because it's available at 1550 on the AM dial in the San Francisco area, but it's also available streaming online and in podcast form. What's special about KYOU is that podcasters actually have a shot at getting their shows on the air! KYOU Radio openly solicits podcasts from the general population to help meet its programming needs.

Figure 2.44

KYOU Radio was the first station in the United States to go all-podcast.

Like NPR in the United States and CBC in Canada, radio stations and networks everywhere are starting to jump on the podcasting bandwagon and are increasingly making content available for download. One of the countless examples is from CHUM Radio in Toronto (**Figure 2.45**). CHUM recently started podcasting its "Roger, Rick, and Marilyn" morning show so that commuters who may have missed the show in the morning can download it at work and listen to it on the drive home.

Figure 2.45

Radio stations everywhere are turning to podcasts to keep connected to their audiences.

This is just one small example of how radio stations are turning to podcasts to reach and expand their audiences. After all, people who work an evening shift normally would not be out of bed in time to listen to a morning show. But if that morning show is available via podcast, they can catch the show on their way to work in the afternoon via their iPod (or other device). If you have a favorite radio program that you can't always listen to, check to see whether a podcast is available for it. You never know.

National Public Radio

www.npr.org

National Public Radio in the United States (**Figure 2.46**) is a prime example of free podcasts that are available to the public. Currently, all the content available for free from NPR is available as streaming content (audio that streams directly for play on a computer-based media player), but not all the files are available as MP3 files yet (although this is changing). Many NPR shows are available for a small charge on Audible.com as well, if you are interested in obtaining a self-contained podcast of a particular show.

Figure 2.46

NPR is a pioneer in podcasting, making many of its shows available via this route.

NPR is an excellent example of radio-show content that is made available to the public so that people can listen to specific shows at their leisure, and as NPR moves to make all of its content available as both MP3 files and streaming content, it can continue to be a leader in the podcasting realm.

To listen to a streaming NPR podcast, you need either the RealAudio media player or Windows Media Player.

Griffin's radio SHARK

In the past five or six years, the DVR (digital video recorder) concept has become reality in hundreds of thousands of homes across North America. DVRs, better known by the name TiVo, allow users to pause, rewind, and fast-forward live television. TiVo units (and their cousins) also allow users to record programs very easily, capturing entire seasons of a show with only a few button clicks. The popularity of TiVo has been so significant that network advertising reps are shaking in their boots!

With the DVR revolution sweeping through Televisionland, you may have wondered why it hasn't swept through Radioland as well. A product from Griffin Technology (www.griffintechnology.com) called the radio SHARK has changed all that. The radio SHARK (**Figure 2.47**) allows time-shifted recording of AM and FM radio signals from your area—that is to say that you can listen to, record, and pause live radio from your listening area.

The radio SHARK, which works on both Macintosh and Windows computers, talks directly to iTunes, turning any new recordings into podcasts that appear in your iTunes window. This is extremely handy; I use mine a great deal to capture local radio shows that I would not be able to catch otherwise. The show is recorded, and within a few seconds, it is transferred to iTunes to be placed on your iPod during the next update.

Figure 2.47
The radio SHARK from Griffin Technology is an awesome podcast-creating tool.

The radio SHARK is extremely flexible. It can be set up to record radio shows one at a time, daily, and even weekly. The software is easy to use and flexible enough to ensure that all the content you want to capture gets captured. The only limitation to the radio SHARK is that you cannot record two programs at the same time. That said, I love mine and recommend it to the world.

Finding Educational Podcasts

It doesn't take a college grad to see that podcasting can easily play a role in improving education. After all, having an entire semester's worth of lectures available as podcasts could greatly improve a student's chances on the final exam.

Duke University

In Chapter 1, I speculated about the future of podcasting and how it might affect education in years to come, but Duke University in North Carolina is already deeply involved in podcasting (**Figure 2.48**).

Duke made headlines in the 2003–04 school year by purchasing iPods for every freshman. These iPods were distributed with an iMic (an iPod accessory that allows for recording, much like an old-fashioned tape recorder) so that students could record lectures as they saw fit. Other classes had lectures recorded as podcasts made available through a special Duke University page in Apple's iTunes Music Store!

This concept intrigued me so much that I contacted Professor Richard Lucic, associate chair of the Department of Computer Science at Duke University, and asked him about this pioneering podcasting project.

Figure 2.48

Duke University leaped to the forefront in educational podcasting, giving an iPod to every freshman during the 2003–04 school year (and every year since).

Farkas: What was the genesis of Duke's iPod program?

Lucic: It was an outgrowth from discussions that the Information Sciences and Information Studies Program at Duke was conducting with Apple to explore incorporating technology in the classroom. The iPod idea came up during these discussions and was expanded to a campuswide program.

Farkas: In a nutshell, how does Duke's program work? Are there microphones in every class so that each lecture is recorded and then turned into a podcast at a central location? Also, are computers supplied for students to download the pertinent podcasts to their iPods?

Lucic: This first year, all freshmen were given iPods, but faculty could also make a request to have any course designated an official iPod course, with loaner iPods given to all students. The freshmen get to keep them; the others have to return them at the end of the class. Students were given an iMic in addition to the iPod so that they could record lectures. Duke's Center for Instructional Technology (CIT) would, on request, come and make a recording of the class, but I think most faculty just made the recordings themselves. Duke made a site available to upload class audio content, and Apple also made a Duke-specific iTunes portal available.

Farkas: What has the impact of this program been in terms of both objective data and subjective feedback? Have the students taken well to this new educational medium?

Lucic: Apparently, the response from both students and faculty was very positive. Duke concluded that incorporating the iPod technology into the classroom did in fact enhance the learning experience. The faculty of the official iPod classes were required to provide feedback from surveys or other vehicles used to poll the students and instructors. Several round-table discussions with faculty and with students were also conducted to assess the subjective feedback. A couple of the key conclusions of the experiment are that the iPods made learning portable, reaching beyond the confines of the classroom; increased student enthusiasm and work quality; and facilitated the learning process.

Duke University Update

I caught up with Professor Lucic for the second edition of this book so that I could ask him about Duke's iPod/podcasting experience since we first chatted a year ago. Here are his responses to my questions.

Farkas: In your opinion, how much of a success has the program been now that there has been some time to refine the subtleties?

Lucic: It appears to be very successful. We are now passing out iPods on a course basis so any student registered for an official iPod course (not just freshmen) gets an iPod, and if they pass the course, they get to keep it. Of course, they only get one iPod even if they take future iPod courses. Over 40 classes are using iPods this semester, and many have incorporated podcasting. Focus groups have been conducted with faculty and students to assess the educational impact of the iPods, and the results have been quite positive.

Farkas: Has the program changed at all in the past 6 to 8 months?

Lucic: The program is now available to all students, not just freshmen. Duke has also significantly expanded the support and tools made available to faculty interested in getting into podcasting. For instance, Duke is working on an open-source podcast management tool called DukeCast that is available to the entire Duke community, faculty, students, student groups, staff, etc. DukeCast makes it incredibly simple to create a podcast, and Duke provides the storage and bandwidth.

Farkas: What are the greatest hurdles still facing the program?

Lucic: One of the biggest problems is intellectual property. It is much harder and more expensive than it should be for some faculty to get access to audio materials for academic purposes in fields such as music or the languages. Other issues include training for students and faculty who are technology-literate, and it does take time. In my case, I feel the results are worth the additional effort, but some of my colleagues are not willing to expend the additional effort.

Farkas: Is video podcasting something that can or will affect the program in the future?

Lucic: I am using video podcasting in my courses. I find it very effective in teaching methods and skills. Other faculty at Duke are using video podcasting in such fields as language education, multimedia communications, art, and drama.

Georgia College & State University

A small school in Milledgeville, Georgia, recently turned to iPods to improve the way its students are educated (**Figure 2.49**). Georgia College & State University has about 5,500 students and around 300 faculty members, but despite its relatively small size, this educational institution is making some big strides in podcasting education.

Figure 2.49

Georgia College & State University has jumped feet first into the podcasting education revolution.

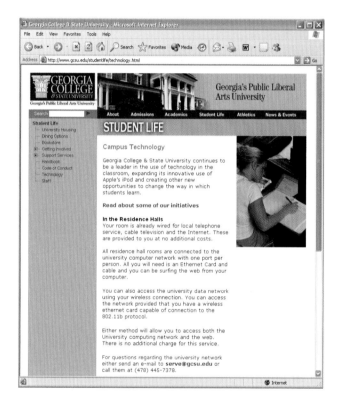

I had a chance to talk with Gregg Kaufman, director of Coverdell Institute at Georgia College & State University, about the school's podcasting initiative.

Farkas: What was the genesis of this program?

Kaufman: The Coverdell Institute serves the Georgia College & State University Academic Affairs Division as a resource for civic engagement and promoting democratic skills that are necessary for becoming a good citizen. Many of the institute's programs provide opportunities for learning outside the classroom. The Georgia College iPod project appealed to me, as iPod technology has many applications for the institute's work with students, faculty, and community citizens. Consequently, I wrote several proposals to the Office of Technology Solutions and met with the staff. The institute was subsequently approved as one of many iPod project leaders at GC.

Farkas: How have the students responded to this concept?

Kaufman: I believe students who take advantage of listening to a guest presentation in their discretionary time appreciate the opportunity. I have heard faculty say that listening to podcasts relative to writing grants and learning about university protocols while commuting is extremely helpful.

Farkas: What are the hurdles in rolling out a project like this? What technical difficulties have you experienced?

Kaufman: We have experienced difficulty capturing the group discussions. It is not possible to record 20 voices with our audio equipment. One of our recent adjustments involves recording the discussion facilitator and one or two participants before and after the discussion, and then creating a podcast to introduce a subject that can be discussed on a blog that extends the weekly discussion.

Farkas: Are there any plans to expand this project?

Kaufman: There are four things in terms of expansion that come to mind immediately:

- A virtual exhibit—visual images and commentary on art and flags that represent America's founding ideas

- A documentary of the Milledgeville mayor's first 100 days in office—film and audio

- Liberty Lectures—podcasts of guest lectures

- A Times Talk podcast and blog—a weekly current-events discussion series "ripped from the *New York Times* headlines."

Medical podcasting

The number of medical podcasts filtering into the directory has been increasing at a steady rate. *The New England Journal of Medicine, JAMA* (Journal of the American Medical Association), the Glasgow Southern Medical Society, the Texas Tech Family Medicine department, and a host of others now have regular medical podcasts for both medical professionals and the general public. I managed to catch up with the two principal characters in one of the most prestigious and famous medical podcasts, "Johns Hopkins Medicine Weekly Health News" (**Figure 2.50**).

The two hosts of this podcast are Elizabeth Tracey, director of "Hopkins Health NewsFeed" (a radio news service program) and Dr. Rick Lange, M.D., chief of clinical cardiology and professor of medicine at the Johns Hopkins School of Medicine.

Farkas: What was the genesis of the podcast? How did the idea come about?

Figure 2.50
There are plenty of medical-related podcasts around, but it's hard to top the "Johns Hopkins Medicine Weekly Health News" podcast.

Tracey: Actually, I thought of the podcast. There was a huge amount of information that started to come out last year about podcasting, including a huge article in *The New York Times*. Since my background is in electronic media and radio, I thought that this would be a no-brainer for us. I'm fortunate enough to work with Rick, who has a very dynamic and engaging personality, and I had already worked with him in the past, so when I ran through my mental Rolodex to think who would be the best fit for this podcast, Rick immediately came to mind.

We decided to look at the latest medical stories and research and then talk about them during the show, because as you know, there is an enormous appetite for this information from the public. There's also an awful lot of misinformation out there, so we thought we could help the situation by presenting accurate information in this format.

Lange: Elizabeth's vision, which I fully grasp, is that it be very timely—for example, what's happened this week—that it be very understandable to the lay audience, that it be conversational and personal, and that we get in on the ground floor of podcasting. While we try to make it conversational and personal, it still is hard science, and that's the foundation of what we do.

Farkas: What to you is the most exciting aspect of podcasting in general?

Lange: The thing that I most enjoy is giving accurate information to a wide audience in a manner that's understandable and enjoyable.

Tracey: I feel extremely fortunate in my job. I get to spend my whole day being stimulated by the literature, but both Rick and I feel that it's our raison d'être to convey this to people in a way that can change their lives. If we can't do that, then it's really just so much fluff with no real import. Also, what I really like about it is that we're getting information out there, so that the next time somebody's confronted with a health problem, they can say, "Hey, I've heard something about this from Johns Hopkins, and I can rely on this opinion." Hopefully, then that person can go to their doctor with that information and use it in their health care plan. That's the real driver for me: to get that information out there so that it has some practical application.

Farkas: What lies in the future for this podcast?

Tracey: This podcast has had an enormous reception, and our numbers are going up constantly—that is, the numbers we can actually track—and we are also getting a lot of press about it. As of right now, we're looking for corporate sponsorship for this podcast, and once that's in place, what we'd like to do is start vodcasting.

Within the institution of Johns Hopkins, we're also doing an enormous amount of podcasting. Everyone wants it on their Web site. For example, right now I'm working with someone on a whole series of short podcasts on various plastic-surgery procedures.

iTunes U

As you can see on Apple's Web site (www.apple.com/education/solutions/itunes_u), iTunes U is a free hosted service for colleges and universities that provides easy access to the institutions' educational content. This content usually includes lectures and interviews (basically, educational podcasts) 24 hours a day, 7 days a week. Apple sees iTunes U as being the most powerful way to manage large amounts of audio or video content and to make it available quickly and easily to students, faculty, and staff. iTunes U is based on the iTunes Music Store software; therefore, it's easy to use. Ultimately, it's not surprising to see Apple jump into the education pond with both feet; the company has always been closely involved with educational programs.

Listening to Podcasts

So now you know where to find and how to obtain your podcasts. How are you going to listen to them? Several options are available to you, depending on what software you are using. First, if you are using a program with a built-in media player, you can enjoy the podcasts on your computer using said player. If you want to use a digital music device, such as an iPod or a Nomad, you must get the podcast downloaded onto your player. There are many ways to do both, as you'll see in this section.

Software-based (computer) players

For those who like to listen to their podcasts directly on their home (or work) computers, a software-based media player is the answer. If the podcast aggregator you are using does not include a built-in media player, and you are not using a program like Apple's iTunes for Mac or Windows, you need to ensure that you have some other form of media player installed on your computer so that you can to listen to the podcasts as they arrive.

Many media players are available in cyberspace. Just about every sound card ever made comes with a media player, as do most video cards, be they from Matrox, NVidia, or ATI. In fact, there are so many media players for Windows-based machines that I could write an entire book on them. Not to worry. Despite the vast array of media players floating around, the ubiquity (and utility) of the "big three" means that I need to discuss only those three options: Windows Media Player, RealPlayer, and QuickTime.

QuickTime

www.apple.com/quicktime
Operating System: Macintosh, Windows

The granddaddy of all media players, QuickTime (**Figure 2.51**) is Apple's entry in the media-player sweepstakes. Introduced in late 1991, QuickTime has evolved and constantly pushed the envelope in doing so. Today, QuickTime is the media player of choice for movie studios when they want to put their trailers out on the World Wide Web. Indeed, QuickTime boasts the highest quality of all of the media players.

Figure 2.51
QuickTime is what the movie studios often use when they put their trailers out on the 'net.

Perhaps the biggest bonus that QuickTime offers is that it is seamlessly integrated into iTunes. Because the majority of digital music devices are iPods, it makes sense that iTunes and QuickTime will be oft-used software in the world of podcasting. The basic version of QuickTime is free, and it does everything a podcast enthusiast needs. The other main factor with QuickTime is quality, and although this is open for debate, few people will dispute that QuickTime is the hands-down winner when it comes to image and sound quality.

RealPlayer

www.real.com

Operating System: Windows, Macintosh, Linux/Unix

RealPlayer (**Figure 2.52**) is the main cog in the RealNetworks wheel. First released in 1995, RealPlayer has long been a favorite of many users, and it arguably has driven many of the innovations in media players. The latest version of RealPlayer, version 10.5, can play CDs, DVDs, audio DVDs, video, and audio, and also allows users to burn CDs. As a bonus, RealPlayer has a TiVo-like feature that allows you to buffer streaming content, such as Internet radio broadcasts. If you dislike Windows Media Player and feel like being closer to the cutting edge, RealPlayer is a good choice.

Figure 2.52

RealPlayer is a very respectable media player.

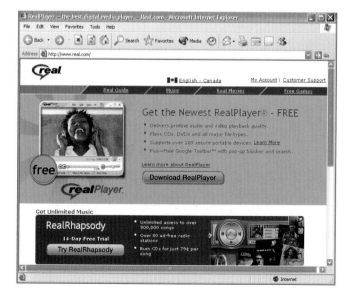

The complaints with regard to RealPlayer revolve around the playback quality of the media (although this is entirely a matter of taste and opinion) and the installation process. If you want to get the latest and greatest from RealNetworks, for example, you must pay for it. We're not against this, but compared with WMP's free status, there are decisions to be made: cutting-edge technology versus cost.

Windows Media Player (WMP)

www.microsoft.com/windows/windowsmedia/default.aspx

Operating System: Windows, Macintosh

Windows Media Player is the default media player from Microsoft Corporation. Because the vast majority of home computers run Windows software, this means that nearly everyone has Windows Media Player (or some version of it) installed. Because this software is free, updates for it can be downloaded at no cost so that users can keep up to date with the latest advances in media-player technology.

The current version of this software is Windows Media Player 10 (**Figure 2.53**), which is available for download at Microsoft's Web site. Windows Media Player can play MP3 files, video files, picture slide shows, and Internet radio, making it a fantastic one-stop basic media player. Don't forget that WMP also plays compact discs, DVD movies, audio DVDs, and MP3 CDs. For Windows users, I recommend Windows Media Player if for no other reason than that you probably already have it on your machine.

Figure 2.53
Windows Media Player 10 in action.

If you update your Windows software regularly with the Automatic Update feature, your version of Windows Media Player will most likely be current.

MP3 players

Although you can listen to podcasts on your computer, the main thrust of the podcasting movement is to make podcasts portable, allowing them to be played on iPods and other digital music devices, including SmartPhones and PDAs. There are more digital music players, Smart-Phones, and PDAs on the market than you can shake a stick at, although in the past 3 years Apple has so thoroughly dominated the field that I must include plenty of Apple products in any analysis of these devices. That said, by sticking to the top few devices in each category, I can give you an idea of what is out there and what the feature sets are.

Before I delve into examining various digital music and video players, however, I need to reinforce the utter dominance of Apple's iPod. According to media reports, at this writing Apple controls more than 80 percent of the total digital music player (MP3 player) market, so I'd be remiss if I didn't focus heavily on these players.

note Although I have included prices for the MP3 players in this section, the market changes so frequently that both prices and model features are likely to have changed (and/or improved) by the time you read this book. This section is intended just to give you a feel for what's out there.

Archos Gmini 500

win **video**

Manufacturer: Archos (www.archos.com)
Price: $699
Memory Type: Hard drive
Memory Size: 40 GB
Weight: 11.2 ounces
Screen: Yes/color (4 inches, 480x272, 262,000 colors)
Battery: Internal/rechargeable
OS Compatibility: Windows XP

The Archos is a high-end portable video, audio, photo, and music player with a stunning 4-inch color screen. The price reflects the high-end nature of this device, but when video podcasting enters the equation, having a larger and brighter screen is important.

The features of the Archos Gmini 500 are as follows:

- 4-inch color screen capable of 480x272 resolution

- Can store up to 160 hours of video

- USB 2.0 connectivity

- Can store up to 400,000 photos or 20,000 songs

- Includes TV output

If a high-end, all-in-one video device is what you're looking for, the Gmini must be considered for its large, crisp color screen, if for no other reason. The addition of plenty of useful features makes it a worthy option, although a very pricey one.

iAudio U2

Manufacturer: COWON America (http://eng.iaudio.com)
Price: $180
Memory Type: Flash
Memory Size: 1 GB
Weight: 1.2 ounces
Screen: Yes
Battery: Internal/rechargeable
OS Compatibility: Macintosh, Windows

COWON America's iAudio U2 digital music player is an excellent flash-based player for both the Mac and Windows operating systems. One of the distinct benefits of the U2 over the iPod shuffle is the inclusion of a screen, although admittedly, the U2 is also larger than the shuffle. The U2 comes with a built-in, rechargeable lithium battery that should give you 18 to 20 hours of playback before the device needs to be recharged.

The U2 comes not only as a 1 GB model, but also in 128 MB, 256 MB, and 512 MB flavors. Following are the prime features of the iAudio U2:

- LCD display

- Personalized logo on LCD display

- USB 2.0 connectivity

iPods, iPods Everywhere

The iPod has dominated the market so thoroughly that it has become a true phenomenon. Perhaps part of Apple's success in this department has to do with the way the iPod has constantly (and quickly) evolved, moving from a 5 GB black-and-white-screened device with an actual wheel on the front to a streamlined 60 GB video iPod that plays music, audiobooks, videos, contact lists, and even photographs. Even since the first edition of this book (in less than a year), three of the iPods mentioned in the first edition are no longer available, and two new models are gracing the shelves! Expect that by the time you read this book, a new iPod model (or two) will be available.

iPod

Manufacturer: Apple (www.apple.com)
Price: $299 or $399
Memory Type: Hard drive
Memory Size: 30 GB (7,500 songs) or 60 GB (15,000 songs)
Weight: 5.5 ounces
Screen: Yes/color (2.5 inches)
Battery: Internal/rechargeable
OS Compatibility: Macintosh, Windows

Photo courtesy of Apple Computer, Inc

The classic-style (that is, the iPods most like the original iPods in design) iPods available at this writing are the 30 GB and 60 GB video iPods. These are the most functional iPods ever created, capable of holding thousands of pictures, movies, video podcasts, music, audiobooks, and contact databases. These are truly monster machines that, despite their huge hard drives and incredible capabilities, are actually smaller than previous iPod generations.

With a very easy-to-use interface that has been copied by its competition, the iPod combines impressive styling with user-friendly features that have propelled it to the top of the heap. The screen on the iPod is a QVGA 320x240 2.5-inch color screen, which makes navigating the menus a treat. The basic features of the iPod are

- Built-in calendar, clock, games

- The ability to make playlists on the fly

- Simple, elegant menu system

- Easy-to-use, multifunction touch wheel

- Rechargeable built-in battery

- Easy plug-and-play compatibility with iTunes on Windows and Macintosh computers

- Capability to play back video and display photographs

- Storage of text files so that the iPod can be used like a PDA for retrieving addresses and other information

- USB 2.0 connectivity

- Compatibility with Audible.com

- Large numbers of accessories, from wired remote controls with FM radio to carrying cases

- Capability to be used as a hard drive on Mac and Windows computers

iPod nano

Manufacturer: Apple (www.apple.com)
Price: $149/$199/$249
Memory Type: Flash
Memory Size: 1 GB (240 songs)/2 GB (500 songs)/4 GB (1,000 songs)
Weight: 1.5 ounces
Screen: Yes/color (1.5 inches)
Battery: Internal/rechargeable
OS Compatibility: Macintosh, Windows

Photo courtesy of Apple Computer, Inc

The iPod nano is an amazing little device. Capable of storing music, audiobooks, podcasts, and contact information, the nano can also be used to store (and display) thousands of digital photographs. Incredibly small and light, the nano is also very tough. When it was first released, someone on the Web tested it by dropping it, throwing it, and eventually running over it with a car, and even after all that, it still worked (although the screen packed it in after the car ran over it).

The iPod nano is the iPod for those folks who value space above all else. Only slightly thicker than a few credit cards stacked together, and only slightly wider than a pack of gum, the nano is a joy to tote around when traveling or exercising. The only limitation is its relatively small storage. If keeping your entire music collection on hand is important to you, the iPod nano shouldn't be your first choice. The nano, however, is the coolest digital music device out there, in my book.

iPod photo

Manufacturer: Apple (www.apple.com)
Price: $349/$449
Memory Type: Hard drive
Memory Size: 30 GB (7,500 songs)/60 GB (15,000 songs)
Weight: 5.9 ounces/6.4 ounces
Screen: Yes/color
Battery: Internal/rechargeable
OS Compatibility: Macintosh, Windows

Note that the iPod photo is still for sale in some places, but it's not actively being manufactured by Apple anymore. The iPod photo is an iPod with the added benefit of a color screen and the ability to store thousands of photographs (in digital form) as well as music. Before you scratch your head wondering why anyone would want to combine these two things, let me point out that the ability to listen to music while a slide show of your latest vacation pictures zips by is surprisingly compelling and enjoyable. With the video/audio output cable, the iPod photo can be turned into a portable slide-show machine, displaying pictures while serenading viewers with music of the operator's choice.

The iPod photo can hold up to 60 GB—more than enough to store a couple hundred CDs and a few thousand of your favorite pictures.

Photo courtesy of Apple Computer, Inc

iPod shuffle

Photo courtesy of Apple Computer, Inc

Manufacturer: Apple (www.apple.com)
Price: $69/$99
Memory Type: Flash
Memory Size: 512 MB (120 songs)/1 GB (240 songs)
Weight: 0.78 ounce
Screen: No
Battery: Internal/rechargeable
OS Compatibility: Macintosh, Windows

The iPod shuffle raised a lot of eyebrows, because it is a flash-memory-based player rather than a hard-drive-driven device. Add to that the fact that the shuffle doesn't have a built-in screen, and it would seem that Apple took a very big risk. Risk or no risk, upon its release, the public immediately fell in love with the iPod shuffle, and waiting lists to buy it were in the 6- to 8-week range!

Despite lacking a screen, the iPod shuffle is an outstanding digital music device that is arguably smaller than a seven-stick pack of chewing gum. The shuffle has the following functions: play, rewind, fast-forward, previous song, next song, pause, volume up/down, and play songs in order or shuffle songs. Although using an MP3 player without a screen as a podcast player may seem strange, I use my iPod shuffle for just that. In iTunes, I transfer two or three podcasts to the shuffle; then it's off to the gym. I strongly recommend that you use iTunes if you are going to purchase a shuffle; only when these two products work together does the iPod shuffle really sing.

tip

Song-count disparity: Why does a Creative Zen Touch with 20 GB of hard-drive space boast that it can hold 10,000 songs when an Apple iPod with the same-size hard drive offers half as much? The answer lies in the details. The number of songs or podcasts that can fit on a digital music device depends entirely on the quality of the recordings you are storing. If you don't mind your songs sounding like they are coming across two tin cans with a wire between them, a 20 GB iPod could hold about 50,000 songs. So remember—look at the size of the hard drive and not the boasts about the number of songs a player can hold. In the case of the players discussed in this chapter, all of them have 20 GB hard drives, and even though the various manufacturers predict that each player can store a certain number of songs, one player will not store more than another, with everything else being equal.

iRiver U10

win

Manufacturer: iRiver (www.iriver.com)
Price: $249.99
Memory Type: Flash
Memory Size: 1 GB
Weight: 2.5 ounces
Screen: Yes/color
Battery: Internal/rechargeable
OS Compatibility: Windows XP

iRiver has moved away from hard-drive-based players and now offers only flash-based players. Its U10 has a very small form factor and fits nicely into the palm of your hand. It has the ability to display photographs, videos, and music, or to play games. Perhaps the most enticing feature of the U10 is its battery life of more than 24 hours—a bonus no matter what kind of player you're talking about.

Available only for Windows PCs, the iRiver has an impressive array of features, including:

- Up to 28 hours of battery life

- 2.2-inch color display

- Built-in FM tuner

- Built-in voice recorder

- USB 2.0 connectivity

When you're shopping for a Windows-based digital music device, you cannot ignore the iRiver U10. The inclusion of an FM radio and a built-in voice recorder automatically save money compared with Apple's iPods, for which those features are available only as add-ons. That said, the U10 has very limited storage space—only 1 GB.

Zen Micro

Manufacturer: Creative (www.creative.com)
Price: $179.99/$199.99/$229.99
Memory Type: Hard drive
Memory Size: 4 G/5 GB/6 GB
Weight: 3.08 ounces
Screen: Yes/monochrome
Battery: Internal/rechargeable
OS Compatibility: Windows

The Zen Micro is a great little MP3 player with tons of functionality. The Micro comes with an FM tuner/recorder so that you can record straight off of FM radio, as well as a built-in voice recorder so that you can record lectures, personal notes, meetings, and the like. Capable of holding contact information and even synchronizing with Microsoft Outlook, the Zen Micro is a great alternative to the iPod.

The downside to the Micro probably is its menu system, which I personally don't find as intuitive as Apple's. But the sound quality is high, there are 10 colors to choose among, and an FM radio (something that costs extra with an iPod) is included, all of which make the Micro a viable alternative.

Zen Vision:M

Manufacturer: Creative (www.creative.com)
Price: $349.99
Memory Type: Hard drive
Memory Size: 30 GB
Weight: 5.75 ounces
Screen: Yes/color (2.5 inches, 320x240)
Battery: Internal/rechargeable
OS Compatibility: Windows XP

The Creative Vision:M claims a 14-hour battery life for a unit that can store 120 hours of movies, tens of thousands of photos, and up to 15,000 songs. Those are some significant boasts, but the Vision:M pulls them off and then some. This is a true challenger to Apple's video iPod, and in some ways, the Vision:M matches up very well, although there are a few shortcomings. The feature list includes

- The ability to create playlists on the fly

- FM radio and built-in recorder

- USB 2.0 connectivity

- Voice recorder

- Built-in personal organizer

- High-definition 2.5-inch color screen

- Vertical touchpad

- Can create movie and photo slide shows, and connect to a TV to display them

The Zen Vision:M has won many industry awards, and I have to say that it's a very impressive unit. The main limitation is the somewhat-clunky interface, but for what you get in terms of value for the money, the Zen Vision:M is an amazing unit.

note Beauty is in the eye of the beholder. Nowhere is that more true than when choosing a digital music player. Because everyone has a different opinion of what looks good and what is easy to use, I strongly suggest that you head to your nearest electronics store and test these units head to head before making a decision.

3

Creating a Podcast

Now that you know what a podcast is, what's it's used for, and how it can affect your life, you may be inspired to create your very own podcast for distribution over the world's podwaves. Perhaps you would love to create a podcast but feel that the technology obstacles preclude you from ever doing so. Or perhaps you aren't worried about the technology but are unwilling to take the time to learn the ropes. Not to worry. Before you succumb to the fear of podcasting technology and crumple up in a fetal position while moaning gently about RSS feeds, have a look at this chapter; it'll change your point of view.

In this chapter, I take a look at the process of creating an audio podcast, from the nuts and bolts of recording techniques to the software that can help you edit and manipulate the podcast. I also include some tips and interviews with podcasting pioneers and aficionados whose hard-won experience will be to your benefit. After covering the equipment and the software needed for podcast creation, I walk you through the creation of a podcast from start to finish, using basic equipment and popular software.

Content

Before you get the ball rolling on creating a podcast, it is critically important to figure out what will be said (or not said) during the show. What limits are there when it comes to choosing content? In short, there are almost no limits to what can be included in podcasts. Podcasting allows you to create shows, dramatizations, vignettes, commentaries, documentaries, and any other content imaginable. Indeed, podcasting is limited only by individual podcasters' imaginations. The sky is the limit, and I encourage you to exercise your creative muscle when brainstorming podcast ideas.

I say there are "almost no limits" on podcast content because some laws dealing with pornography, threatening political leaders, and other such nastiness would preclude anyone from including such material in a podcast. Despite the fact that podcasting is a new medium with a wide-open feel, it is not a license to break the law. It's only a matter of time before someone crosses a legal line with a podcast; just make sure that someone is not you.

Before the Podcast

This section deals with everything relating to the creation of podcast content, from outlining a show's content to booking guests and formulating questions for them. Although it is possible for a podcaster just to pick up a microphone and create a "show," it requires a much larger effort to ensure that the podcast sounds professional while being a compelling listen. In this section, you see what you can do *before* the tape is rolling to maximize the quality and enjoyability of your podcast.

Some podcasts are clearly created by the seat of the host's pants, with little regard to a structure or plan for entertaining or educating the listener. But the "amateur" moniker that is attached to podcasting doesn't mean that the content of podcasts needn't be professional.

Interview with Steve Mirsky of
Scientific American Magazine

Steve Mirsky (**Figure 3.1**) is an editor of *Scientific American* magazine. He also writes the magazine's "Antigravity" column. A freelance contributor to numerous other publications, Mirsky became a science writer after being awarded an AAAS Mass Media Fellowship in 1985. He was a Knight Science Journalism Fellow at the Massachusetts Institute of Technology during the 2003–04 academic year.

Photo with permission of Ellis Mirsky.

Figure 3.1
Steve Mirsky.

Farkas: Whose idea was it to move to a podcast format? What inspired *Scientific American* to move into this area?

Mirsky: Actually, it was upper management that came to the online editor, Kate Wong, with the idea of moving into the area of podcasting. Kate's the editor of the *Sciam* online operation, and the podcast is considered to be part of the Web site. Kate knew that I had a background in radio, and she came to me to create the podcasts.

Farkas: What was/is your role in creating the podcast? Do you manage all aspects from content to editing?

Mirsky: I'm it, actually. I do everything from recording the interviews, to editing the content, to writing the dialogue, to polishing the podcast for broadcast.

Farkas: What process occurs in terms of finding content for each podcast?

Mirsky: Each podcast contains four elements. The lead interview is related to content or the author of an article in the current issue of *Scientific American,* or a member of the staff who's been to a scientific conference, for example. Then I try to have one interview that's a little bit on the lighter side and one more that's not necessarily related to content in the magazine; it might be from the science headlines that week. I also include a segment entitled "Totally Bogus," which is a fun quiz game where the listener must choose which one of four science stories from the last week is untrue.

Farkas: Is there anything you'd like to say about the technical side of podcast creation?

Mirsky: I know that I really notice it on other podcasts when the audio quality of the person on the telephone is very fuzzy and filled with static. I actually run my voice feed and the interviewee's feed through separate channels so that I can use the Magix Audio

(continued on next page)

Interview with Steve Mirsky of
Scientific American Magazine *(continued)*

Cleaning Lab software to clean up the individual tracks to remove any hum or hiss. I clean each track individually, adjust the volumes, mix the tracks, and then clean the mix again. I hit on this technique after a few podcasts, and it really improved the sound quality.

Farkas: Is video podcasting something that might appear in the future for *Sciam?*

Mirsky: I know the magazine has expressed an interest in doing something along those lines in the near future, but it hasn't evolved beyond that yet.

Farkas: Are there any oddities about podcasting you'd like to comment on?

Mirsky: Well, we changed the name of the podcast (**Figure 3.2**) after seven episodes. Originally, it was called "The *Scientific American* Podcast," but it wouldn't come up if you searched the word *science.* So we changed our show to "Science Talk: The Podcasts of *Scientific American* Magazine." So as a piece of advice to podcasters out there, you have to be careful what you name your show, or it may not show up in searches by your target audience.

Figure 3.2

The podcast page of *Scientific American* magazine.

With a little bit of background work, one can turn amateur hour into something that is respectable and highly listenable.

There are four key elements to a successful preproduction process for a podcast:

- Draft a document that establishes the general tone, taste, and attitude of the podcast.

- Establish the topic of the show, the length of the show, and any guests who will join you.

- Create a general outline for the show, breaking content into blocks no longer than 5 minutes each.

- Construct a detailed script to keep the show well paced and to ensure that the host(s) and any guests who are being interviewed always have something to talk about. (If you are good at speaking on your feet, this step may not be necessary.)

note **This section details the creation of an audio podcast, but most of the same principles apply to video podcasts. Check out Chapter 4 for information on creating video podcasts.**

Mission statement

The first thing to do is write a mission statement or design document that sets out rules for the tone and overall structure of the show. This document should spell out the boundaries of taste with regard to language, touchy topics (politics, abortion, favorite ice creams), and the overall attitude the host(s) should exhibit.

Although this process may seem rigid for an amateur podcast, the act of going through it goes a long way toward solidifying the overall feel of the podcast in your mind. Remember, this document is not set in stone; you can change it as much or as little as you want. The important thing is to establish the ground rules before you get your pearly whites in front of the microphone. Knowing the general rules allows the host to be more natural and to enjoy the process rather than sweat over the appropriateness or validity of everything he or she is saying.

Recording Telephone Interviews

Recording a telephone interview may seem like an insurmountable challenge, but fortunately, several inexpensive devices allow you to record telephone conversations directly from the phone line. I need to point out that these devices are illegal in some places without the consent of the person on the other end of the phone, so you need to inform your interview subjects at the beginning of the conversation that they are being recorded.

Several phone recorders plug into the phone line between the phone's receiver and base unit; others plug into any phone jack in the house. These little devices often cost less than $10. For purposes of recording telephone interviews, I suggest the Radio Shack Recorder Control (**Figure 3.3**). At $25, this device will automatically start to record telephone conversations when the receiver is picked up. Keep in mind that this device does not include the recorder itself; it's just the conduit from the phone line to the recording device.

Figure 3.3
The Radio Shack Recorder Control allows you to record telephone interviews.

When recording a telephone conversation, it's best to use a digital recorder that you can attach to your PC or Mac; that way, you can upload the file to your computer easily.

Topics, guests, and show length

I'm guessing that you've already established an overall concept for your show, but even though you think "Foot Care for Firewalkers" is a fascinating theme for a podcast, you still need a topic for the first show.

I strongly suggest that you choose a topic for the show and stick to it, keeping as much of the content centered on the theme as possible. If you title your podcast "Navel-Gazing for Experts: To the Hole and Back," be sure to stay focused on the topic throughout. People who "tune in" to the podcast have done so because they have read the title and synopsis of the podcast. It is likely that listeners will be disappointed if the podcast strays too far from the announced concepts. It is advisable to make a reference list of related topics so that in the heat of the podcast, you can keep the show on track with just a glance or two at the topic list.

Double-Ender Interviews

Occasionally, the opportunity to interview someone by phone or even in person will arise before the podcast is set to be recorded. Often, it can be difficult to set up an interview during the podcast recording time, so the interview/conversation is recorded ahead of time. In the realm of radio and television, an interview that is conducted in two parts, with the interviewer's questions being added later, is called a *double-ender* (**Figure 3.4**), and this technique can be used successfully by podcasters and professional television reporters alike.

Figure 3.4
In a double-ender interview, both sides of the interview are recorded separately and pieced together later.

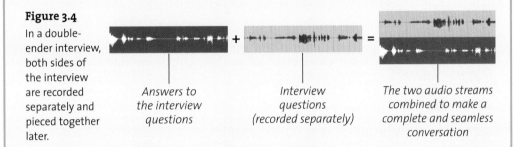

Answers to the interview questions

Interview questions (recorded separately)

The two audio streams combined to make a complete and seamless conversation

A double-ender may occur when you want an interview with someone in another city, but you prefer for the interview to sound live rather than tinny, as though it were coming off a phone line (which is your other alternative). In this case, you need to get a friend or someone near the interviewee's location to meet with that person and record the interview there with relatively high-quality equipment. Then, when the file arrives, you record your own voice asking the questions and ultimately put the two together to make it seem like a live interview in which you are directly asking the interviewee the questions!

In the world of podcasting, the practice of recording double-ender interviews is usually done to improve the quality of the interview. After the interview is recorded, you can re-record your voice asking the questions, and you can even choose not to run some of the guest's answers during the podcast. In short, using double-ender interviews gives you more control of the quality and content of your podcast.

Next up, you need to choose who, if anyone, will be a guest on your show. Guests are fantastic; they provide instant content, and you can bounce ideas and humorous anecdotes off them. The important thing to remember when getting a guest for your podcast is to have at the very least a crude list of questions before the podcast begins. A guest might be a good friend whom you can chat with for hours, but once the mikes are on, it's a different ball of wax. Having a nice list of eight or ten questions at the ready will ensure that even if your stressed-out mind draws a blank, the show will go on!

Last, you must decide on a length for the show. Initially, shorter is better; you would be surprised how hard it can be to fill even one half-hour the first time you attempt to create a podcast.

Outline

Now that you know what the podcast is about, what the tone of the show is, and how long the podcast is, it's time to put together an outline that breaks the show into segments no greater than 5 minutes long. As shown in **Figure 3.5**, the outline should be set up in such a way as to help you fill every minute of your podcast with entertaining and/or interesting content.

Figure 3.5
An outline is a valuable tool to help keep you on track during a podcast.

If your outline for a 20-minute show is broken into two 10-minute segments, there isn't much point in constructing it. On the other hand, if the outline is broken into 10 two-minute segments, the flow and content of the show will be easy to maintain. Even if you have a detailed outline, and a guest takes five times longer to answer a question than you thought she would, the outline is still valuable, because all the show segments are in front of you, allowing you to decide at a glance which ones to drop.

In summary, an outline helps remove any indecision during the recording of the podcast. When the host has a written schedule sitting on a desk in front of him during the recording, any unexpected happenings don't have to fluster him or cause other problems.

 note

If your show is meant to be a spontaneous affair, a script is most certainly not for you. That said, even if your podcast is meant to be spontaneous, packed with seat-of-the-pants observations, an outline is still worth the effort.

Detailed script

If the outline is complete enough, a detailed script may not be necessary. The need for a script depends on the host's ability to talk on the fly and keep the flow of the show going. If the host is the kind of person who has difficulty with idle banter while maintaining the flow of the podcast, however, a detailed script will be in order.

A script can be so detailed that it contains every line that is to be said during the show (**Figure 3.6**), but if you go to this extreme, you must be careful not to make what's being said too rigid. We have all seen movies in which the lines seem scripted, as though they are just being read and not formed naturally by the actors. In radio, you want a similar feeling—a natural feeling that gives the illusion that everything that's being said is spontaneous.

Figure 3.6

The script for the first "Secrets of Podcasting" podcast was written out entirely (except for the banter with the guest). I used color coding in the text blocks to help me know where I was and what sections represented new concepts.

Secrets of Podcasting Script

Hello and welcome to the Secrets of Podcasting: Audio Blogging for the Masses podcast. I'm the author, Bart Farkas, and I'd like to start out by saying yes, that really is my name.

There's actually a funny story there. At one point I was working for one particular publisher and I was writing quite a few books in a short period of time. The rival publisher, seeing the name 'Bart Farkas' thought that it was a pseudonym that my publisher was using as a catch-all for in-house authors. A couple years later when I called the rival publisher to discuss a book deal, they were absolutely flabbergasted to learn that I was indeed a real person!

Anyhow, I'd like to thank you for listening to this brief podcast, during which I'll give you a brief look at the content of the Secrets of Podcasting book, and how best you can use it to create a better podcast on your own time. I'd also be checking in with Rich Doperalski of the Rich and AJ show, a podcast that has been around since the early days of podcasting. Of course, in that case the early days of podcasting could reasonably be considered to have been 30 months ago, but given us the Rich and AJ show is an old timer of sorts.

Podcasting is a phenomenon that started just over a year ago and has grown at an unbelievable rate. Since the term podcasting was coined and the realm of podcasting has expanded and morphed repeatedly, making it difficult to keep up with all of the changes.

Indeed, that was one of the challenges with writing the book. After all, the process of writing a book, moving it through the editorial process, and then get it printed and out into stores inherently takes weeks, and in the case of Podcasting even a few weeks can mean that significant changes have occurred.

For example, since the book went to press Virgin Atlantic announced that it is now making guided-tour podcasts for those folks who book flights on their airline. This way, when you land in a city, say, Paris, you can have a guided-tour podcast that takes you through the louvre, or on a tour of the city's main attractions, complete with background information. Obviously there are a few limitations to this, but it's still a great idea and I can imagine an iPod with a built-in GPS and color screen that gives guided tours all over the world. Guided tours already work very well in places like the Forbidden City in Beijing, and on the island of Alcatraz, so using podcasts to increase the flexibility and power of these tours makes perfect sense indeed.

Before I get to my esteemed guest, I'd like to talk about our book, Secrets of Podcasting Audio Blogging for the Masses, published by Peachpit Press in Berkeley California.

Equipment

One great thing about audio podcasting is that you can do it at home with a basic Mac or PC and an inexpensive microphone (which may even come with the computer). High-end equipment is nice, to be sure, but many of the best podcasts out there are recorded and edited with basic equipment and widely available software.

Still, there are several ways to set up a podcast recording "studio," from using nothing more than a computer with a microphone to having high-end microphones, preamps, digital recorders, and the like in a sound-dampened room.

For serious podcasters, the list of necessary equipment is as follows:

- Microphone

- Preamp

- Digital recorder (or computer)

- Headphones

- Sound-editing software

This section examines the equipment you need to get up and running (software is covered a little later on). I need to point out that many devices can make podcasting easier or higher quality, but I cannot cover every one of them in this book. Instead, I examine several key pieces of equipment in each category.

Microphones

Arguably the most important device in the creation of an audio podcast, the microphone stands between your voice and the podcast file. As such, it behooves you to ensure that the quality of the recording is as good as it can be, based on your budget and expectations.

Two main types of microphones are used for podcasting: condenser microphones and dynamic microphones.

Condenser microphones use a capacitor to capture sound. This works when the pressure from the sound changes the space between the thin membranes in the capacitor. The advantage of a condenser microphone is that it has a very broad frequency response; the down side is that it requires a source of power (such as a battery) to charge the capacitor so that it can work.

note

Condenser microphones require external power to function. This power often comes from a preamp device and is referred to as *phantom power*.

Dynamic microphones work by measuring the movement of a wire coil around a magnetic field as the sound waves agitate the wire. The advantages of a dynamic microphone are that it is cheaper to make than a condenser microphone and can be miniaturized more easily. The down side is that the frequency response isn't as good as that of a condenser microphone, making the sound quality inferior.

tip

Condenser microphones sport significantly better fidelity than dynamic microphones, but this also makes them more prone to crackling, background noise, and *P*-popping (the tendency for words starting with the letter *P* to make a popping sound when spoken). Fortunately, there are ways to eliminate these problems; see the "Popping *P*s" sidebar later in this chapter. Condenser microphones also require power, which often must be supplied by a preamp device (adding around $100 to the cost).

Omnidirectional or Cardioid?

Although the decision to go with a dynamic or condenser microphone may be easy, that isn't the only decision that faces the buyer. Most microphones are either *omnidirectional* (sound enters the microphone equally from any direction and can be picked up with equal fidelity no matter where it comes from) or *cardioid* (sound is picked up mostly from in front of the microphone).

As a general rule, cardioid microphones are used for radio, but in most cases an omnidirectional microphone can do the job admirably for podcasting, especially if the podcasts are recorded with several guests gathering around one microphone.

If the frequency response (quality of sound) is important to you, I recommend a condenser microphone. Most microphones that come with computers are dynamic microphones, and although they are acceptable, you will have to purchase a quality microphone eventually if you want your podcasts to sound professional.

Apple Computer built-in microphones
Frequency Response: Varies
Power: Internal

Many Apple computers come with a built-in microphone (**Figure 3.7**). The newest iMacs have a microphone (and/or camera) in their screens, and many older Macs come with an external microphone that can be plugged in. Although these microphones do not offer super-high quality, and although there can be some issues with the computer's fan sound getting picked up, these built-in microphones can do the job in a pinch.

Figure 3.7

This image of an iBook G4 shows the built-in microphone to the right of the screen.

Photo courtesy of Apple Computer, Inc

Built-in microphone

Audio Technica ATM73A-SP
Frequency Response: 25 Hz–17,000 Hz
Power: Battery

This headset cardioid condenser microphone is best used by those who want to create podcasts as a one-man (or one-woman) show. At $120, the ATM73A-SP (**Figure 3.8**) isn't inexpensive, but it is a high-quality microphone that you can clip to your head so that you don't have to worry about being directly in front of it all the time.

Figure 3.8

A headset-based cardioid condenser microphone is a great choice for a lone podcaster.

Behringer C-1
Frequency Response: 40 Hz–18,000 Hz
Power: Phantom

The Behringer C-1 (**Figure 3.9**) is a professional-quality condenser microphone that uses a cardioid pattern to accept sound. At around $55, the C-1 is an outstanding microphone for the beginning, intermediate, or even expert podcaster. The real bonus is that the quality is high but the price is surprisingly reasonable for a product of this caliber.

Figure 3.9

The Behringer C-1 condenser microphone is an awesome value and can more than do the job.

Photo © Copyright 2005. BEHRINGER Spezielle Studiotechnik GmbH.

Blue Microphones Snowball
Frequency Response: 40 Hz–18,000 Hz
Power: USB port

The Snowball (**Figure 3.10**) is a condenser microphone from Blue Microphones, and it's aimed more or less directly at the podcasting crowd. Although the Snowball has had some mixed reviews, it is a decent high-end (for simple home use) microphone for podcasters. One thing that I particularly like about the Snowball is its look; it's a great mix of modern and retro styling, making it like a piece of art on your desk!

Figure 3.10

You've just gotta love the look of the Snowball.

DT 234 PRO Microphone
Frequency Response: 20 Hz–18,000 Hz
Power: Phantom

This headset cardioid microphone costs around $99. Made by Industrial Audio Software, the DT 234 (**Figure 3.11**) contains a dynamic transducer, meaning that the quality is ultimately not as robust as that of a condenser microphone. That said, the DT 234 is a comfortable and reasonable performer best used by podcasters who do their work alone and don't have to share their microphones frequently.

Figure 3.11

The DT 234 headset-based cardioid dynamic microphone.

Electrovoice 635A

Frequency Response: 40 Hz–18,000 Hz
Power: Phantom

The Electrovoice 635A microphone (**Figure 3.12**) is probably the best-known microphone in the TV and radio business. A very dependable (some would say nearly indestructible) microphone, the 635A is a mainstay in the radio business and will serve any podcaster well, especially if recording on the road is in the cards.

Figure 3.12

The Electrovoice 635A is a mainstay microphone and, according to Tod Maffin, is the "best microphone you can buy when starting out."

Griffin LapelMic

Frequency Response: 100 Hz–15,000 Hz
Power: Passive

When it comes to portable microphones for off-site recording, the Griffin LapelMic (**Figure 3.13**) is one of the best solutions, and at $10, it's pretty hard to beat. Not only is it a stereo microphone, but it's also very small, and it works with virtually any recording device. If you're recording a lecture or one-half of a double-ender interview, pin the LapelMic to the subject's chest area, and start recording!

Figure 3.13

The LapelMic is an excellent portable stereo microphone for recording on the fly.

Heil Sound PR 40
Frequency Response: 28 Hz–18,000 Hz
Power: None

The Heil Sound PR 40 (**Figure 3.14**) is the high-end microphone I'm recommending for the very serious podcaster. At $325, the PR 40 isn't cheap, but it's unbelievably economical when you consider that the sound quality is comparable to that of microphones that cost hundreds (or even thousands) of dollars more. The PR 40 ships in a custom cherry wood box and comes with a mount assembly. If you are serious about the mount, a spider mount is also available. For those serious podcasters who want a high-end microphone without the high-end cost, this is the answer.

Figure 3.14
The PR 40 provides high-end performance at a midrange price. It's my choice for a high-end microphone.

Labtec Desk Mic 534
Frequency Response: 100 Hz–16,000 Hz
Power: 1.5 V DC (supplied through connector cable)

I include this microphone (**Figure 3.15**) because it is a very common device that is included with many PC bundles. As a result, many 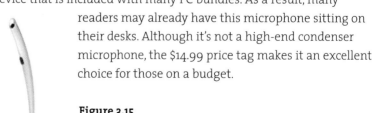 readers may already have this microphone sitting on their desks. Although it's not a high-end condenser microphone, the $14.99 price tag makes it an excellent choice for those on a budget.

Figure 3.15
It's very low cost, but for beginners, this microphone can do the job.

Logitech USB Headset 250

Frequency Response: Headset: 20 Hz–20,000 Hz

Microphone: 100 Hz–16,000 Hz

Power: USB port

Priced at $39.99, the Logitech USB Headset 250 (**Figure 3.16**) is a good choice for those who are willing to forgo the highest sound quality in exchange for mobility and ease of use. The Headset 250 plugs into the USB port of your computer and is easy to set up. The microphone is a dynamic noise-canceling device that strives to filter out background noise. The result can be a mellowing of the user's voice, but it is a small price to pay, considering what you are getting for your money with this product. The Headset 250 can be used on either a Mac running OS X or a PC running Windows 98SE, 2000, Me, or XP.

Figure 3.16

A low-cost but effective headset microphone, the Logitech USB 250 is a solid option.

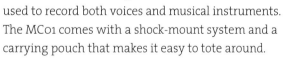

note Logitech (www.logitech.com) has one of the largest selections of microphones for computers offered by any manufacturer. If you are looking for a microphone specifically for your PC, and you don't want to shop around, Logitech offers a huge variety.

MC01 Professional Condenser Microphone

Frequency Response: 30 Hz–16,000 Hz

Power: Phantom

The MC01 (**Figure 3.17**) is the microphone for the high-end user (relatively speaking). At $180, the MC01 is designed for studio use and can be used to record both voices and musical instruments. The MC01 comes with a shock-mount system and a carrying pouch that makes it easy to tote around.

Figure 3.17

The MC01 Professional Condenser Microphone is a quality high-end microphone.

Stageworks CC12

Frequency Response: 40 Hz–18,000 Hz

Power: Phantom

The Stageworks CC12 (**Figure 3.18**) is a more-than-suitable condenser microphone that is comparable to the Behringer C-1 in many ways. The CC12 uses a supercardioid pattern to accept sound and, as such, produces very clear sound capturing. Although it lists at $99, the Stageworks CC12 condenser microphone is widely available for around $50.

Figure 3.18

Like the Behringer C-1 microphone, the Stageworks CC12 offers high quality for a low price.

> **tip**
>
> Radio Shack (www.radioshack.com) also has a wide selection of decent microphones that can be used for podcasting. Two examples are the Pro-Unidirectional Dynamic Microphone and the Headset Microphone with Gooseneck Boom. Both of these are very good microphones (for the price) and retail for $29.97.

Audio interfaces/preamps

Many of the microphones mentioned in this chapter require phantom power—that is, they require a device to supply power to them so that they can work. These devices can't be plugged straight into the computer; instead, they must be connected to a preamp device that acts as an input controller between the sound input devices and your computer.

Although these devices add another layer of cost to your podcast setup, they are not terribly expensive, and they also allow access to several extra features you probably didn't even consider. Preamps offer

Popping *P*s

One of the major problems for first-time podcasters is that any time they say the letter *P*, it comes across as a popping sound. This sound is created when the exhaled air used to form the *P* hits the microphone, temporarily overwhelming it. Unfortunately, this sound is not something that you can remove or doctor with editing software; after it's recorded, it's there forever. Not to worry, however. If podcasting is becoming a major part of your life, there are two relatively simple solutions:

1. Run out and buy a pop filter like the OnStage ASVS6GB Microphone Pop Filter ($25.94; **Figure 3.19**).

2. Stretch some pantyhose over something that is hollow and roughly circular. An old coat hanger that has been bent into a circle will do just fine. Tod Maffin suggests using an embroidery hoop for this purpose, and at a cost of about $2, it's not a bad alternative!

Figure 3.19
The OnStage ASVS6GB Microphone Pop Filter is an inexpensive way to avoid popping your *P*s.

When the pop filter/screen is ready to go, you must set it up so that it is right in front of the microphone. If you have purchased a commercial pop filter, there is likely a clamp that does this for you. If you have made your own pop filter, you must come up with your own creative solution. A pop filter can be hung from the roof; it can be attached to a small lamp; heck, it can even be placed around your neck on a harmonica holder so that no matter where you are, the pop filter is always there!

No matter how you solve the problem, getting a pop filter in front of the microphone ensures that the sound entering the microphone is clean and unaffected by the "wind" forces associated with normal speech.

the ability to input any sort of sound into your computer, including inputs from a musical instrument (like an electric guitar) or even inputs from an old eight-track tape that you want to convert to an MP3 file. In short, a preamp computer device allows the input of virtually any kind of audio signal. For everything from making podcasts to recording an acoustic guitar track for GarageBand (a music-creation program for the Macintosh), a preamp is a wise investment.

note Every preamp device mentioned in this section is capable of accepting any audio signal for conversion to a digital music or data file. For this reason, these are excellent tools for converting old audio tapes or vinyl records to MP3 files or music CDs.

Behringer Eurorack UB802

The Behringer Eurorack UB802 (**Figure 3.20**) is a preamp/mixer that defies logic when one considers what one is getting for the price. At a paltry $49, the UB802 includes

- Two studio-grade Invisible Mic Preamps (IMPs)

- Three-band equalizer on all channels

- Six balanced high-headroom line inputs

- One postfader effects send per channel for external effects devices

- Tape inputs assignable to main mix

- Main mix outputs plus separate control room, headphones, and stereo tape outputs

- External power supply for noise-free audio

- Switchable phantom power for condenser microphones

Figure 3.20

The Behringer Eurorack UB802 is the "must have" preamp/mixer for budget-conscious (and otherwise) podcasters.

For the price, the UB802 has a very impressive wow factor, and it's my personal choice for anyone who wants a very capable and expandable preamp. If growing your podcast and adding features and layers are important to you, this is the best preamp for the money on the market.

Behringer Tube Ultragain MIC200

The Behringer Tube Ultragain MIC200 (**Figure 3.21**) is a preamp that's perfect for live and hard-disk recording applications (such as creating a podcast). The great thing about the MIC200 is that it uses vacuum tubes, which create a warmer sound and make the device a great match for condenser microphones. The MIC200 includes 16 distinct preamp effects that are designed for everything from drums to vocals. At $60, the price is right. The one caveat about the functionality of this powerful device is that it does not have a USB connector, making it more difficult to connect to a PC or Mac than other preamps are.

Figure 3.21

The Behringer MIC200 is a solid preamp that uses old-fashioned vacuum-tube technology.

Griffin iMic

The iMic (**Figure 3.22**) is a USB device that functions as a universal audio adapter. With the iMic, you can connect any sound input (including microphones) to any Mac or Windows computer with a USB port. Because the iMic is so easy to use, and because it also supports line-level output for speakers or an external recording device, it's the perfect match for podcasters. At $39.99, it is one of the best—and least expensive—units available.

Figure 3.22

The iMic is a low-cost, yet effective, solution.

The benefit of USB audio input devices (preamps) comes from the fact that the inputs are isolated from any electronic "noise" that might otherwise be picked up from a computer's sound card. How much of a difference a USB device makes isn't entirely clear, but in the case of the iMic, it works like a charm.

M-Audio MobilePre USB

At $159, the MobilePre USB from M-Audio (**Figure 3.23**) is an outstanding preamp for both the Mac and PC platforms. The MobilePre USB has two channels, stereo microphone input, a powered headphone monitor, phantom power, stereo line outputs, and a gain switch. It's an easy-to-use, powerful preamp that will more than suffice for most podcasters (in fact, it's what I use).

Figure 3.23
The M-Audio MobilePre USB is a solid preamp for both the Mac and PC.

Although designed specifically for use on laptops in mobile situations, this little preamp is plenty powerful enough to sit proudly in any home studio.

M-Audio Podcast Factory All-in-One Solution

This chapter looks at microphones, software, and preamps separately, but M-Audio recently released Podcast Factory (**Figure 3.24**), a complete, USB-powered podcasting solution for both Macintosh and Windows computers. The package includes everything you need to create a podcast:

- Professional 24-bit/48 kHz audio interface

- Dynamic broadcast microphone with stand

- Software for creating the podcast (Abelton Live Lite 5)

- Stereo headphone and output jacks

- RSS feed creation software

- Sound effects and music loops from multiple genres

Figure 3.24
Podcast Factory from M-Audio is an all-in-one podcast-creation package for less than $200.

For those who want one-stop shopping for creating podcasts, the M-Audio Podcast Factory is an excellent choice. For $179.99, you get everything you need to create high-quality podcasts.

PowerWave USB

With a price tag of $99, Griffin Technology's PowerWave USB (**Figure 3.25**) falls between its sibling, the iMic, and M-Audio's MobilePre USB. Like the other units, the PowerWave USB is capable of receiving input from any microphone while importing it to the PC or Mac it's connected to. The PowerWave also includes an amplifier to drive monitor speakers and is powered by the USB port.

Figure 3.25
The PowerWave USB is Griffin Technology's high-end audio input device.

XPSound XP202

The XPSound XP202 (**Figure 3.26**) is the Cadillac of USB audio preamps. Workable on both the Mac and PC, the XP202 includes a phono preamp as well as a mic preamp for recording voice and other live perform-ances. The XP202 includes a USB connection and a built-in sound card for processing information right on board.

At $199, this is not the inexpensive alternative, but for anyone who wants more control of the sound input process, the XP202 is the right machine for the job. The feature list includes

- USB interface

- 24-bit operation

- Two microphone inputs

- One headphone amplifier (onboard)

- Mix/balance control

Figure 3.26
The XP202 is the high-end preamp for podcasters who want the best.

Although I tout the XP202 as a high-end preamp, there are plenty of very-high-end preamps on the market that cost hundreds and even thousands of dollars.

Headphones

Headphones can be considered a luxury, but when it gets down to brass tacks, you will quickly find that a decent pair of headphones is more of a necessity. You cannot monitor the podcast during the actual recording unless you have headphones, for example. If the podcast were playing back through your computer's speakers as you were recording it, a noisy feedback buzz would be the result. For this reason, it is important to get a pair of headphones that is at the very least comfortable for you to have on your head while creating your podcasting masterpiece.

This section suggests several quality headphones for your consideration, but ultimately, any headphone that you are comfortable with will do. If you already own headphones—even MP3 player headphones—they will do the trick. There are literally hundreds of headphone models out there, so all I can recommend is that you use a set that sounds good to you and is comfortable. Of course, if you already are using one of the microphones with attached headphones, you can skip this section.

JVC HA-G55 Headphones

The JVC HA-G55 headphones (**Figure 3.27**) are a middle-of-the-road choice priced at $55. With a frequency response of 12 Hz to 25,000 Hz, they are capable of delivering a wide range of sounds to your ears. The advantage of the HA-G55 is the full-size, deep-bass ear cups that create a rich sound that encircles the listener. These headphones are another excellent choice.

Figure 3.27

Priced between the two Sony models mentioned in this section, the JVC HA-G55 headphones are a quality option.

Sony MDR-V150 Headphones

At $19.99, Sony's MDR-V150 headphones (**Figure 3.28**) are a quality yet inexpensive option from a well-known manufacturer. They are comfortable over-ear headphones with 30mm drivers and ferrite magnets for exceptional response (for the price).

Figure 3.28

Despite being a very basic set of head-phones, the Sony MDR-V150 model is good enough for the beginner.

Sony MDR-V700DJ Headphones

This is a midlevel set of headphones from Sony. The sound quality of the MDR-V700DJ headphones (**Figure 3.29**) is noticeably better than that of the cheaper Sony 'phones, so for those who insist on high fidelity, these are a great choice. The V700DJ is a disk-jockey model with swivel ear cups, allowing the wearer to flick the cups over to permit conventional hearing. Many podcasters like this feature when they are engaging in an interview (they like to have one of their ears exposed).

At $149.99, these headphones aren't cheap, but the sound-fidelity difference is noticeable.

Figure 3.29

These DJ headphones feature swivel ear cups.

Noise-canceling headphones

Although all headphones are based on pretty much the same premise, a relatively new kind of headphone takes portable audio to a new level. The noise-canceling headphone has made a big splash in the past 5 years, giving consumers the ability to listen to their favorite music while effectively shutting out outside noise. The technology behind noise-canceling headphones is amazing, to say the least, but all you need to know is that they really work, and the results can be nothing short of startling. I take a look at two pairs of noise-canceling headphones in this section: one for a larger purse and one for those on a budget.

 tip Always try noise-canceling headphones before you buy them. Many of them have an annoying buzz that's created by the noise-cancellation circuit. This buzz is certainly distracting, and there's no way to tell which models or brands have it without trying them first.

Bose QuietComfort 2 Headphones

The Cadillac of noise-cancellation headphones, the Bose QuietComfort 2 (**Figure 3.30**) headphones feature excellent comfort, superb noise cancellation, and reasonable sound quality. The price, however, is on the high side, at $299.

Figure 3.30

The Bose QuietComfort 2 headphones are considered by many people to be the best.

Philips HN 110 Noise-Canceling Headphones

The Philips HN 110 noise-canceling headphones (**Figure 3.31**) are the first choice of Steve Mirsky of *Scientific American* magazine, inter-

Figure 3.31

The Philips HN 110 is a great pair of noise-cancellation headphones for the money.

viewed earlier in this chapter. For the money ($99), they are an excellent alternative to the rather pricey $299 Bose QuietComfort 2 headphones. Some would argue that the Philips headphones offer better sound and equal noise cancellation, although it's subjective enough that I won't guess at which one is actually better.

Digital recorders

Although it may be tempting to rush out and purchase a digital recorder for your podcast needs, I need to point out that your computer itself is a powerful digital recorder, and the need for one of these devices is certainly not critical as long as you have a Mac or a Windows PC. Still, digital recorders do have a certain amount of *je ne sais quoi* that makes them more glamorous.

Of course, there are legitimate reasons to get a digital recorder, not the least of which is the portability these devices afford the user. A digital recorder allows you to record programs virtually anywhere, provided that you have a microphone (some digital recorders have built-in microphones) and power to drive the unit. The only limitation with a digital recorder is its memory size; high-quality digital recordings take up a lot of memory space, so the size of the memory in a recorder is the main limiting factor when it comes to recording.

In this section, I take a look at five digital-recorder options: a trio of high-end digital recorders, a midrange MP3 player option, and an iPod using Griffin Technology's iTalk microphone. The digital-recorder market offers plenty of choice, and it isn't within the scope of this book to examine them all, but taking a look at the cost and features of several units can help fill in the blanks about digital recorders and the need (or lack thereof) to own one.

note Although I suggest a few digital recorders in this section, it's important to point out that virtually any MP3 player with the ability to record from a microphone input and then export the file to a PC or Mac can be used as a digital recorder. If you own an MP3 player, you may already have a portable digital recorder and not even know it. Either way, the selection of MP3 players that can record in this manner is vast, giving the buyer plenty of choice.

Apple iPod with Griffin iTalk

  Not long after the first iPods were released, some iPod owners who were fooling around with the iPod's interface discovered a hidden menu that implied that the iPod could be used for voice recording. It turns out that these folks had stumbled onto something that would show up about a year later: devices designed to record directly onto the iPod's hard drive. Today, Griffin Technology offers the iTalk, a small device that attaches to the top of the iPod photo as well as to third- and fourth-generation iPods.

note The iPod mini and nano don't have recording abilities built into their firmware, so the Griffin recording devices work only on third-generation, fourth-generation, and photo iPods. The iTalk currently doesn't work on video iPods, either, because of the difference in the smart jack between older iPods and video iPods.

The iTalk (**Figure 3.32**) is an ingenious device that attaches cleanly to the top of the iPod, and after you install the software (which is easy to do), the iPod becomes a competent voice recorder. The iTalk comes with a built-in speaker that allows you to record without any other equipment, but if quality is your goal, I suggest plugging an external microphone into the iTalk.

Figure 3.32

The iTalk is a mobile-recording option for iPod users.

The iTalk will record on the iPod's hard drive in WAV file format. When the iPod docks with iTunes, the file will be transferred to iTunes automatically, making it easy to pull off for editing.

The device does have a down side, in that the user cannot change the recording bit rate. Also, the quality of the built-in speaker, although decent, is not exactly broadcast quality. Still, as a portable recording device, the iTalk is an inexpensive ($49) option for an iPod owner.

 Belkin (www.belkin.com) also sells a voice-recorder attachment for iPods, as well as a microphone attachment for the same purpose. The Belkin Voice Recorder for iPod works on all iPods except the mini, nano, and video iPod.

Edirol R-1

  The Edirol R-1 (**Figure 3.33**) is one example of a high-end digital recorder. Although there certainly are more elaborate (and expensive) recorders on the market, this unit (at a price of around $500) is my choice at the high end. The R-1 is a handheld 24-bit digital recorder that is capable of recording high-quality broadcasts virtually anywhere.

The feature list of this product is very impressive:

Figure 3.33
The Edirol R-1 is one example of a high-end digital recorder.

- 137-minute MP3 (compressed) recording time (with built-in 64 MB memory card)

- 24-bit uncompressed recording

- Dual built-in omnidirectional microphones

- External microphone input

- Line inputs

- 13 internal digital effects

- Built-in equalizer

- Built-in tuner (to tune musical instruments)

- Built-in metronome

- USB 2.0 connectivity

Clearly, the Edirol R-1 is a full-featured digital recorder that exceeds the needs of most podcasters. For anyone who is looking to become a serious podcaster, the Edirol is worth considering. Its many built-in features, the high quality of its recordings, and its portability make it a very popular choice.

iRiver IFP-795

The iRiver IFP-795 (**Figure 3.34**) is a tiny (512 MB) MP3 player that can play for up to 40 hours on 1 AA battery. At $129.99, the IFP-795 is reasonably priced for a flash MP3 player, but it is much more than just that. Weighing in at just under an ounce and a half, the IFP-795 is a surprisingly full-functioned digital recorder, complete with a separate line input for an external microphone.

Figure 3.34
The iRiver IFP-795 is an amazingly functional digital recorder that doubles as an MP3 player.

Because the iRiver comes with software that allows easy connectivity to PCs or Macs, its USB 2.0 connection makes connection and export of recorded files a breeze. The device supports recording bit rates between 8 Kbps and 320 Kbps in WMA, MP3, and OGG music formats.

Marantz PMD660

The Marantz PMD660 (**Figure 3.35**) is small enough to fit in your hand, but it still has plenty of features that make it a favorite of podcasters everywhere. Many of the podcasters I talk to use Marantz digital recorders to create their podcasts.

Figure 3.35
The Marantz PMD660 is a popular choice for serious podcasters.

The PMD660 records 16-bit PCM WAV files at 44.1 kHz or 48 kHz and has the following features:

- Can record stereo MP3 files at 128 Kbps

- 1 GB CompactFlash card can hold more than 1 hour of uncompressed stereo

- Operates for 4 hours on 4 AA batteries

- Stereo in/out lines

- USB 2.0 interface

- Optional wired remote control

- Two built-in condenser microphones for stereo recordings in the field

Marantz digital recorders continue to be popular in the podcasting set, and I don't see that changing in the near future. The PMD660 is a great choice for those who create regular podcasts and want high quality and mobility at the same time. The PMD660 lists at $699, but it's routinely available for $499.

M-Audio MicroTrack 24/96

The M-Audio MicroTrack 24/96 (**Figure 3.36**) is an example of a very rugged and versatile two-channel mobile digital recorder. The MicroTrack can record both WAV and MP3 files to CompactFlash and includes high-fidelity microphone preamps with phantom power for studio-quality microphones. Via a USB 2.0 connection, files on the MicroTrack's CompactFlash cards can be dragged to both the Mac and PC. The battery is an internal lithium-ion type that recharges when the unit is connected to a USB port. At $499.95, the MicroTrack is priced in line with similar models.

Figure 3.36

The MicroTrack 24/96 is a solid and rugged solution for mobile podcasting; it's perfect for a home studio as well.

Interview with Tree House Concerts

Podcasting's reach is so vast and diverse that I am constantly amazed at how it's being used. I came across a great podcast by a group called Tree House Concerts (www.tree houseconcerts.org; **Figure 3.37**) and had a chance to chat with the founder, Greg Pool.

Figure 3.37

The Web site for Tree House Concerts.

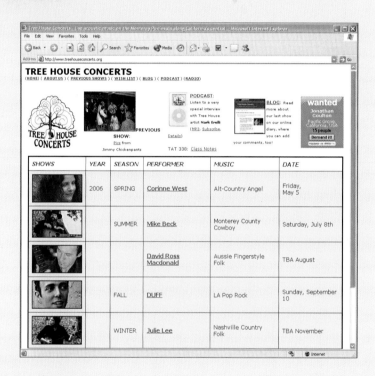

Farkas: Tell us about Tree House Concerts. How did you get started? What's the underlying philosophy?

Pool: My wife, Juliet, and I got tired of the 45-minute drive north to Santa Cruz to see live music. In 2003 we began a house-concert series as a way to bring a Celtic band out from Boston, at their suggestion. From there, I've taken pity on artists who have played locally in clubs but to paltry audiences. Juliet and I knew that between each other's circle of friends, we could easily draw 30 folks out for a night of live acoustic music every other month. Now, with a brand-new baby daughter, it makes it very convenient to have the music come to us.

Interview with Tree House Concerts *(continued)*

Farkas: When did you first think that the podcasting medium suited this format?

Pool: The Tree House Concerts podcast is a mix of after-show interviews, recorded right after performances, and album reviews of artists I couldn't book because of scheduling conflicts.

With respect to the interviews, I realized that my audience might want to hear more from the artists, and more often than not, the artists were hanging around after the show anyway, chatting away. I knew that if I could capture some of our conversations after the show, it would be valuable in extending my brand, if not the artist's brand as well. And not everyone can come to a house concert, so this was a way of saving them something from the night and keeping them interested in the next concert.

Farkas: In what nontraditional ways do you see podcasting moving, especially in your niche?

Pool: I think an after-show interview with the artist becomes a valuable tool for the artist's self-promotion, and being able to link to it makes it easy to add to the artist's Web site. And for an emerging artist, sometimes it's the only way to get visibility in the iTunes Music Store, searching on their name and finding this podcast.

Farkas: Have there been any technical issues with recording high-fidelity music for podcasts?

Pool: I've stayed away from trying to record the evening's music, just because it's enough responsibility to host the evening. And it's easy enough to sample off an artist's CD to mix in clips with the interview.

Farkas: What do you see in the future for Tree House Concerts?

Pool: I'd like to get out of the house and record interviews with artists at clubs, especially ones that have played my house and are returning to the area. I'd also like to do more album reviews and phone interviews. I just recorded a Skype interview with Mark Erelli, in support of his new album. Mark played only our second concert in 2004. And although the licensing is an issue, I would like to play more podsafe music (for example, Creative Commons) on a regular basis, especially for emerging artists.

Farkas: Will video podcasting play a role in Tree House Concerts in the future?

Pool: Most likely not, only because I don't think it adds to the interview or conversation, and it's one more piece of technology to set up after the concert is over.

Software

Part of what makes podcasting so appealing and so popular is the fact that it can be done relatively simply with a user's existing computer and accessories. After the audio podcast file has been recorded, it is still a good idea to use sound editing software to remove any imperfections and insert some appropriate background music. Fortunately, *plenty* of quality shareware and freeware programs are available to help you do just that.

It is also important to note that most sound-editing software can also be used as a digital recorder. In fact, many podcasts are created with a microphone that came with the computer, inputting directly into a program like Audacity or GarageBand. Many sound-editing programs are available, and increasingly, a new type of all-in-one program is showing up. These programs, like iPodcast Producer and Sparks, allow the user to create a podcast from start to finish and even publish the podcast, all from one program!

In this section, I examine several quality sound-editing/recording programs for the Mac, Linux, and Windows environments. I include freeware, shareware, and commercial products, some of which are limited to sound recording and editing; others are one-stop options that allow you to create a podcast and publish it without ever leaving the program.

Ogg Vorbis

Often referred to as just *OGG*, Ogg Vorbis is an open and free audio compression format. Vorbis was created after Fraunhofer-Gesellschaft announced plans to charge licensing fees for the MP3 file format in 1998. It was then that Chris Montgomery began work on the project. The codec was released in July 2002, and the Ogg Vorbis compression format was born.

Slowly but surely, the Ogg Vorbis format is making inroads in the world of audio sound compression. In the past couple of years, it has shown up increasingly on the Internet, in podcasts, and even in some commercial video games. Ogg Vorbis enthusiasts claim that the quality of an OGG is higher than that of an MP3 file, but I can't tell much of a difference. I'll leave that part up to you.

Adobe Audition 2.0

win

Adobe Audition (**Figure 3.38**) is a high-end professional sound editing/recording suite that offers advanced audio editing, mixing, and sound processing capabilities. This software is aimed mainly at professionals, but at $349, it is not priced outside the range of a serious podcaster. It certainly isn't hyperbole to say that Adobe Audition 2.0 contains myriad features that a podcaster is likely never to use, but for those mavens who want every possible capability at their fingertips, this software is a great value for the money.

Figure 3.38

Adobe Audition is one of the best choices for those who want high-end sound editing when creating a podcast.

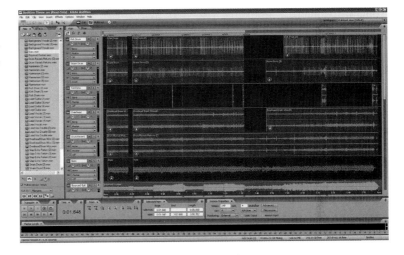

Audition's feature list is so long that it might take up several pages in this book, so I'll stick to the highlights as they pertain to the realm of podcasting:

- All-in-one application for mixing, creating, editing, and adding audio effects

- Can be used to edit video soundtracks

- More than 50 digital signal processing tools and effects

- Up to 128 stereo tracks

- Up to 32 inputs with an equalizer on every track

- Audio scrubbing to scan through audio quickly

- Can record, edit, and mix high-resolution 32-bit files at sample rates up to 192 KHz (double the quality of DVD audio)

- Audio restoration features that allow you to clean up poor recordings

- New mastering tools

- Multichannel encoder for creating 5.1 surround sound (six speakers: center, left, and right front; left and right rear; and subwoofer)

Although it clearly isn't for the weekend podcaster who wants to create relatively simple programs, Adobe Audition 2.0 is inexpensive enough that hard-core podcasters can enjoy its massive suite of features. You can download a trial version at www.adobe.com.

Audacity

Audacity is the program of choice for many podcasters, in part because it is free, but mostly because it's a fantastic, powerful, easy-to-use program. Audacity can be used to record podcasts (with an attached microphone) or to edit existing sound files. Available for Mac computers, Windows PCs, and Linux PCs, Audacity is freeware and is so powerful that it most likely puts a dent in the sales figures of other programs that are for sale. You can download the program from http://audacity.sourceforge.net/download for each of the three operating systems (**Figure 3.39**).

As often occurs in the world of the Internet and computing, this freeware program is superior to some of the for-sale programs on the market. In the realm of podcasting, Audacity has quickly risen to be the top dog for audio mixing and recording (when recording directly on a PC or Mac).

The deep feature list for Audacity includes these items:

- Can record from microphone, line input, or other sources

- Can create multitrack recordings and dub over existing tracks

- Can record up to 16 channels at the same time (special hardware required)

Figure 3.39

Audacity is available for most computer users, be they Mac OS, Linux, or Windows inspired.

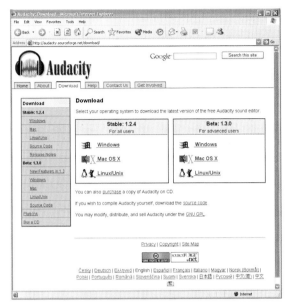

- Can import WAV, AIFF, AU, and Ogg Vorbis files

- Can import and export MP3 files

- Easy cut-and-paste editing

- Volume fade in/out feature

- Built-in effects generator, including echo and phaser sounds

- Can record at up to 96 KHz (more than double a music CD's quality)

- Upgradable with plug-ins

Audacity is such a complete and easy-to-use recording/editing tool that it is my first choice for all three platforms. There are lots of programs out there, but for someone who is just starting out on a tight budget, free is a great price to pay, and Audacity is also a fantastic piece of software.

tip

Because Audacity is such a great piece of software, I recommend that if you use it as your primary editing/recording program, you donate some money to support the development of the next generation of the program. This goes for all freeware. It doesn't matter whether you donate $1 or $100; if you use the software a great deal, donating to the developer is the right thing to do.

Audio Cleaning Lab 10

Audio Cleaning Lab 10 (**Figure 3.40**) is a commercial program that has several indispensable tools for managing podcast audio streams. Audio Cleaning Lab 10 is available for purchase and as a demo from Magix's Web site (www.magix.net). Lab 10 has some outstanding features that make it indispensable for podcasters.

Figure 3.40

Audio Cleaning Lab 10 is an amazing piece of software for cleaning up the audio quality of your podcasts.

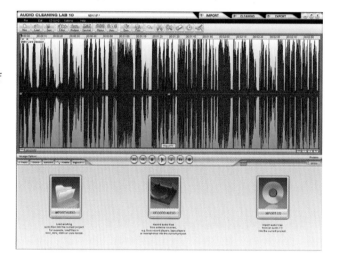

The feature list includes

- Chorus effect—adds body to thin-sounding recordings

- Spectral Cleaning—removes background noise from the recording without audibly influencing the output signal

- DeNoiser 2.0—removes hisses, hums, and background whistle noises

- DeHisser 2.0—minimizes background hiss

- Capability to burn up to seven full-length music CDs onto a single DVD at the same quality

- Task Assistant with built-in video clips to help you learn the nuances of the software

- Surround Editor—allows you to edit surround sound to your specifications

Perhaps the most powerful and useful features are Spectral Cleaning, DeNoiser 2.0, and DeHisser 2.0, all of which allow you to clean up static-filled or fuzzy-sounding interviews that you conducted on the telephone. The results are truly amazing. Magix Audio Cleaning Lab 10 is only $39.99—well worth the money for what it does.

BlogMatrix Sparks! 2.0

Sparks! 2.0 is an all-in-one solution for the Mac and the Windows PC, making it very simple to create a podcast and publish it without ever leaving the program. Sparks! 2.0 is a podcast aggregator as well as an audio recorder, editor, and podcast publisher. It's free for most of the features, but if you want to use the recording feature, you must pay a $10 fee (although the recording feature comes with a 30-day free trial).

Sparks! is truly a one-stop solution for podcasters and podcast listeners. The feature list for this software is very impressive:

- Records and edits podcasts

- Publishes podcasts with ease

- Acts as a podcast aggregator (**Figure 3.41**)

- Acts as an Internet radio portal

Figure 3.41

Sparks! 2.0 acts as a very functional podcast aggregator, if need be.

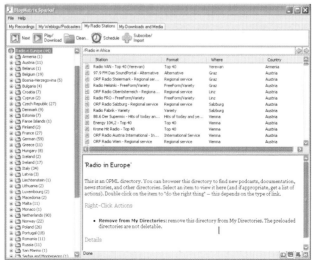

- Acts as a blog reader

- Allows the creation of podcasts from Internet radio and other sources

- Can use multiple tracks and import music to create podcasts

As a one-stop shop, Sparks! 2.0 is an impressive piece of software. For true podcasting aficionados, I suspect that Sparks! 2.0 won't satisfy completely, but for the casual podcaster or the podcaster who just wants to create occasional podcasts, Sparks! is an excellent solution.

 tip If creating a regular podcast is your goal, BlogMatrix also sells packages for publishing podcasts. These services run between $5 and $100 per month, depending on the level of service one needs. Check out Chapter 5 for details on how to use BlogMatrix Sparks! 2.0 to publish podcasts on the World Wide Web.

Interview with Evo Terra and Michael R. Mennenga

Evo Terra and **Michael R. Mennenga** are hosts of the top-15 podcast "Slice of Sci-Fi" (**Figure 3.42**).

Farkas: When did you first become aware of podcasting?

E & M: On October 12, 2004, my [Terra's] partner sent me a link to a page where Doc Searls was talking about DIY radio with this new thing called podcasting. Two days later, and I am neither [kidding] you nor making this up, I hacked our RSS feed and figured out how to use the <enclosure> plug-in in MovableType. My response back to him contained words like "this could potentially change how we do things," and it did. A day or two later, we got listed on Podcast Alley.

Farkas: What made you decide to create your own podcast?

Figure 3.42
"Slice of Sci-Fi" is one of Evo and Michael's podcasting creations.

Interview with Evo Terra and Michael R. Mennenga *(continued)*

E & M: We've been producing audio content for distribution on the Web and through terrestrial radio stations since February of 2002 and had enjoyed a fair amount of success. But terrestrial radio isn't our best market, and it was frustrating to try to explain what our show was all about and why a station should carry us.

When we got booted last year from the No. 1 AM talk-radio station in town because we were *too popular* and causing a "speed bump" in their all-right-wing-politics-all-the-time format, we realized there had to be a better way to reach people who wanted to listen to our content, which likely didn't fit in with any radio station's lineup. Podcasting was that method.

Farkas: What has surprised you the most with regard to the impact of your podcast(s)?

E & M: The immediacy, quality, and quantity of the feedback. We reached tens, if not hundreds, of thousands of listeners on our broadcast shows. Maybe once a week, we'd get an e-mail from them. Oh, sure, our phone banks were lit up each time our live call-in show was on, but our syndicated show rarely got us an e-mail or even a comment on the Web site.

However, from the moment we started releasing our show via podcast, the e-mails and Web-site comments started coming. It's as if the podcatchers feel more of an emotional attachment to our show. Maybe that's because it's still not easy to listen to a show. With that kind of investment, you want the show to be the way you want it, so you're not afraid to let the talent know your feelings.

Farkas: Technically speaking, what was the most difficult thing about getting a podcast off the ground (so to speak)?

E & M: Personally, we think listening to a podcast is more difficult than making one. People who want to make a podcast have the motivation to figure it out, but people who might want to listen are quickly turned off by all the hoops. That's the biggest stumbling block right now for the whole movement.

For podcasters, the problem lies in understanding the RSS feed. Recording a show is intuitive. I push the red button and talk, right? FTPing the file isn't hard, as it's no different than moving files from one spot to another on your computer. The challenge is RSS. Yeah, there are lots of tools to automate the process, but inasmuch as some software sucks at what it's supposed to do, RSS feeds need to be tweaked at the code level in order to make them as effective as possible.

Follow-Up Interview with Evo Terra

Evo (**Figure 3.43**) tends to infect others with the podcasting bug. His latest and perhaps most ambitious project is Podiobooks.com, an online "library" of freely available books released in serialized podcast form.

Farkas: In the last interview, you said that the biggest problem for people lies in understanding the RSS feed. Do you believe that this situation has improved? If so, what has improved it?

Terra: I know I stand in the minority with my opinion. Many very smart and influential people see RSS in the same light as SMTP, the set of rules and formats that make e-mail work. Everyone uses e-mail, but few know the deep inner workings of it.

Figure 3.43
Evo Terra.

I see RSS as different. Yes, it handles distribution much like SMTP handles e-mail, but it also handles presentation, an attribute I feel is as critical as ID3 tagging or the quality of your media file. Simple tweaks and modification to the RSS file can significantly increase the "usability" by the end user. Sure, there are some great services like FeedBurner that make it easy to get a "compliant" RSS feed, and I highly recommend them. But to make effective changes to the presentation of your media files, you need to have the ability to edit and control your RSS feed from the source. I'm not suggesting you create a feed by hand. That's silly. But I am suggesting that minor modifications to certain elements in a feed can make a big difference.

Farkas: What do you think of the rise of video podcasting? What will its place be?

Terra: I love video podcasts and subscribe to seven right now. They are inherently less consumable for me, as I don't always have the time to devote my eyes as well as my ears to the moment. But I do think that video podcasts will allow a whole new batch of creative people the opportunity to hone their craft. Scrapbooking parties were all the rage a few years back. I wonder if we'll see "vidcast" parties popping up?

Farkas: Where is podcasting going in the next 2 years?

Terra: In about 20,000 different directions! Sure, there will be standards and conventions many will follow. You'll see more and more corporations dipping their toes in the water and a few making good headway.

I'm most excited about new applications for podcasting technology. We've seen a handful of these emerge so far, like DailySonic, which allows you to create custom podcasting

Follow-Up Interview with Evo Terra *(continued)*

content on the fly. Or what we're doing at Podiobooks.com, where we customize each RSS feed to each user, allowing our members to start any book from the very first chapter and chose their own distribution cycle. I'm sure there are other innovative thinkers out there busy bending the podcasting model to fit previously unfilled needs.

Farkas: What's the single best piece of software for podcasters that has emerged in the past year?

Terra: iTunes with podcasting support. Surprised by my answer? Let's face it—there are some really great tools to help people create podcasts. But it wasn't that hard to begin with. I have nothing against lowering that bar further, but it's still way too hard to subscribe to podcasts. iTunes changed that overnight, which is why most of us show 70 to 80 percent of our subscribers using iTunes.

GarageBand

Folks who own Macintosh computers likely have a copy of GarageBand (**Figure 3.44**) already sitting on their hard drives. If for some reason GarageBand has eluded you, it is included with all new Macintosh computers and can be purchased with iLife '06 for $79.99 ($99.99 for a five-computer family pack). What makes GarageBand so appealing to Macintosh enthusiasts is the way in which it interacts with iTunes, iWeb, and Mac OS X. Like most Apple applications, GarageBand's ease of use is very impressive, allowing a first-time user to put together an impressive multitrack recording in only a few minutes. As of this writing, GarageBand is up to version 3.01.

Figure 3.44

If you own a Mac, there's a good chance that you already own GarageBand, the only sound recorder/editor you'll need.

GarageBand's ease of use comes from simple audio-track creation, drag-and-drop editing, and the ability to add music or other audio files simply by dragging them out of iTunes. GarageBand also allows users to create their own musical instruments or input live musical instruments. Although GarageBand was originally designed specifically for the creation of music, the inclusion of iWeb and various tools specifically for podcast creation make it an elegant solution that works seamlessly with the rest of the software on your Macintosh when creating podcasts.

GarageBand's features include

- Multitrack recording

- Point-and-click editing

- Compatibility with iTunes and the iLife '06 suite

- Multiple voice effects

- Complete control of all aspects of recording, including timing and pitch

iPodcast Producer

iPodcast Producer (iPP; **Figure 3.45**) is a commercial product that runs $149.95 from Industrial Audio Software. iPP is meant exclusively to be a tool for recording, editing, and then publishing podcasts. The product is not as slick as Audacity or GarageBand, but it does contain the features necessary for getting the job done.

iPP contains a sound/music recorder with two tracks (one for voice and one for music), a fader, and the ability to add up to 12 music or sound effects to

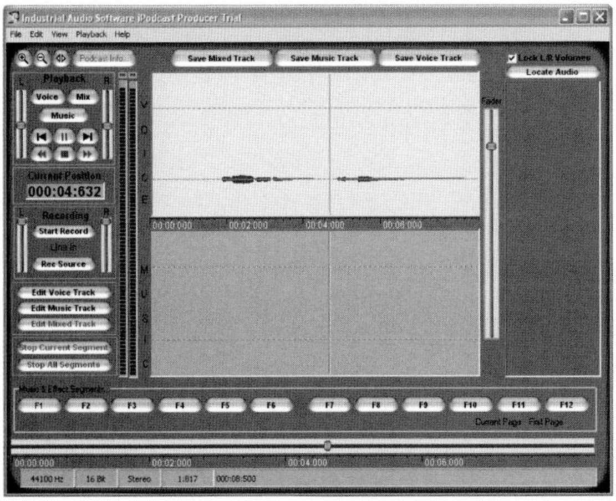

Figure 3.45
iPodcast Producer is a competent piece of software but a little pricey, considering what is available for free.

keys F1 through F12 on the keyboard. After you assign a sound to one of these keys, you can insert that sound into a recording dynamically by pressing the key that activates it. The recorder also allows for importing other audio sources in WAV or MP3 file format.

After recording, you can access the iPP Editor and edit or modify the sound files with digital effects. You can apply 19 different effects to recordings during this process. When the file is complete, IPP allows the newly created podcast to be syndicated right from the program. If you don't already have a spot to save your file for the RSS feed, Industrial Audio Software can sell you space starting at $49.95 per month.

Propaganda

Like iPodcast Producer, Propaganda (**Figure 3.46**) is designed to be a one-stop podcast-creation station, allowing the user to create, edit, and publish podcasts with relative ease. Propaganda has a free 14-day trial; the cost to keep using it after that is $49.95.

Figure 3.46

Propaganda is a one-stop podcast-creation package for Windows computers.

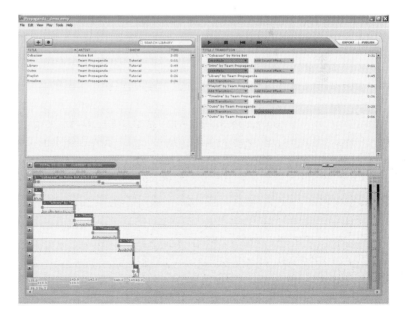

The feature list of Propaganda includes

- One-touch recording

- Recording from microphone or portable digital recorders

- On-screen VU meters

- Ability to rearrange clips in any order

- Ability to add background music and sounds

- Fade in/out transitions

- Ability to publish completed podcasts directly to a Web site

Propaganda allows you to record a podcast from a microphone and to organize and edit the voice file while adding background music and audio effects. When the podcast is complete, Propaganda allows you to upload the show to an RSS feed for distribution on the World Wide Web. If a one-stop piece of software appeals to you, Propaganda is an acceptable alternative for creating and publishing podcasts.

Sound Byte

Sound Byte is a bit of a different animal from the other software packages discussed in this section, because it does not directly help you create podcasts or publish them; instead, it works as a computerized cart machine. In radio stations of the past, a *cart machine* was a device that held a large number of cartridges with short audio blurbs, commercials, sounds, and other such material. When the DJ needed a particular sound, he or she could press a button, and that sound would come off the cartridge and get played on the air. This was a way for radio stations to add unique sounds to broadcasts, and it worked pretty well.

Sound Byte (**Figure 3.47**), from Black Cat Systems, costs $24 (after a free trial) and effectively duplicates those old radio cartridge systems with the digital equivalent. The palette comes with 75 slots, each of which is capable of holding a distinct sound byte, piece of music, or sound effect (or whatever you want). When you're recording a podcast, you can simply click one of the sound effects to insert that effect into the background.

Figure 3.47

Sound Byte allows you to create a palette of sounds that you can access with a click of the mouse.

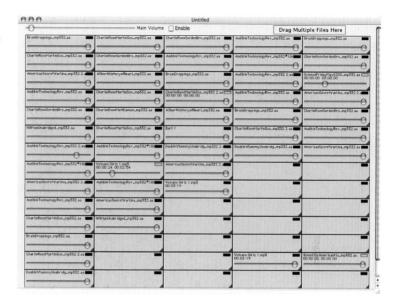

For podcasters who like to fly by the seat of their pants and add sound effects as needed, Sound Byte is an outstanding tool. Sound Byte is available only for the Macintosh at this point, but it is a valuable tool that certain podcasters appreciate and use.

Sound Forge 8.0

Sony's Sound Forge 8.0 (**Figure 3.48**) is another piece of software that allows you to work on either audio or video podcasts. It contains a powerful audio recorder coupled with a superior editor that allows for easy cutting and pasting, mixing, crossfades, and effect application. Sound Forge also comes with built-in music loops that make it an all-in-one stop for every audio aspect of a podcast.

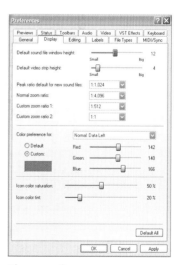

Figure 3.48

Every aspect of Sound Forge 8.0 can be tweaked.

The feature list of Sound Forge 8.0 includes

- Audio recorder and editor

- Professional audio effects

- Extensive video support, including more than 40 professional studio effects for video

- Audio restoration tools

- Highly configurable

At $299.99, Sound Forge 8.0 isn't for the budget-conscious podcaster, but for those who want serious power and the ability to do a lot with one package, Sony has the software. You can download a limited 30-day free trial from www.sonymediasoftware.com.

Sound Recorder

There are many freeware, shareware, donationware, and commercial sound recorders on the market, but Windows users need not go any farther than their Start menu to find an audio recorder that can do the job. In Windows XP, you can find Sound Recorder (**Figure 3.49**) in this path: Start > Programs > Accessories > Entertainment > Sound Recorder.

Figure 3.49
Sound Recorder is free, and it's sitting right there in Windows.

Sound Recorder is limited in that it records only in mono, in 8 bits at 22 kHz, but for some podcasts, that level of quality is enough to get by. Amazingly, this little utility contains an Effects menu that allows you to increase or decrease the clip's speed, add an echo to the clip, or even reverse the clip's direction. This may be your chance to resurrect the "Paul is dead" controversy!

Sound Recording and Editing Tips

Much of the skill you develop in creating podcasts will come with experience. No matter how much you know about the various terms and aspects of software packages and hardware, in the end, the most important thing is *doing*. That said, there *are* a few important tips that will help you when you are recording, editing, and mixing your podcast:

- When recording, try to use your normal voice. Many people attempt a "radio" voice, and it comes off sounding fake or contrived. Practice talking in your normal voice to help your first podcast come off better.

- First-time podcasters often speak too loudly into the microphone. It's important not only to speak at a conversational level, but also to be careful not to vary the volume of your voice or the distance between your mouth and the microphone a great deal. Doing either of these things will result in an uneven podcast in which your voice will "drop out" or "explode" during the show.

- Use a pop filter (also known as a pop screen) in front of the microphone to eliminate pops when saying the letters *P, B,* and *F.* See the "Popping *P*s" sidebar earlier in this chapter.

- When recording, make sure that the levels don't go over the zero-decibel mark on the DB meter. If that happens, the high end of the recording will get clipped off, resulting in very poor sound quality.

- Record at the highest sampling rate possible. CD quality is 44.1 kHz; DVD quality is 96.1 kHz. It's important to record at the highest quality that your recording device will allow. When you're using a small digital recorder, the size of the memory stick is the usual limiting factor. On a computer, however, there is usually enough hard drive space to record at any level.

- If you are going to use commercial music in your podcasts for any reason, you must get an appropriate license for it (see "Legalities" later in this chapter). Most music is licensed by ASCAP or BMI, and both organizations offer licenses for podcasters.

- When interviewing a guest, don't be afraid to rerecord your questions, especially if the questions didn't come off right in the first place (for example, you were coughing or stammering while

Getting Started: Advice from Phil Torrone

Phillip Torrone is an author, artist, and engineer based in Seattle and is associate editor of MAKE:, as well as an Internet-strategy analyst for creative firm Fallon Worldwide, best known for its award-winning work on BMW Films.

Farkas: What do you recommend (hardware and software) for the beginning podcaster?

Torrone: If you have a Mac with GarageBand and a Griffin iTalk or a USB microphone, the results will be surprisingly professional. On a PC, any powered microphone and Audacity will get you started. I've found that a portable recorder tends to get you in the podcasting zone more than sitting in front of a computer. If you're going somewhere, actually interviewing someone, there's a lot more context and richness in the audio than the mouse clicks and keystrokes.

Farkas: How has podcasting helped you personally with regard to your career/business?

Torrone: I started podcasting early on, so it's helped a lot in terms of being considered an "expert" in the arena. There have been a lot of opportunities to pursue businesses in podcasting, but I've been more interested in spreading the word about how to create them with writings, how-to articles, and other efforts. To me, that's the exciting thing: turning on tons of people to the self-publishing of audio.

Farkas: What are your top five tips for a beginning podcaster?

Torrone:

1. Get a good microphone. USB; it doesn't matter—something that sounds good will make any podcast a lot better.

2. Try before you buy. A lot of podcasters go out and buy a lot of gear the pros use. Try experimenting with what you have first. In the end, the big spend might not matter.

3. Love or hate your topics. Passion comes across really well in audio; stick to the stuff you care about or despise. Both make great podcasts.

4. Break eggs. Make mistakes; try different gear; try different encodings. Don't spend too much time getting it "right"—just get it out there, and the rest will follow.

5. Use Creative Commons (see "Creative Commons" later in this chapter). License your works with a Creative Commons license. Not only is it good for you, but it's also good to get more people aware of the CC.

asking the question). It's easy to rerecord the question and place it over the original question. The listener need never know.

- Use a fade-in and fade-out at the beginning and end of the podcast. This small touch gives a very impressive feel to the show and makes the proceedings come across as being professional.

- Include background music during the podcast (see "Legalities" later in this chapter). Background music can be used in several ways. First, it can demarcate different phases or sections of the podcast, rising to signify the passing of a segment and falling off again to signify the beginning of a new topic or to introduce a guest. Second, music can and should open and close a show, with several seconds of music preceding and following the first and last things said by the host.

Music

Music is a very important part of podcasting. After all, many podcasts are like terrestrial radio broadcasts, in that they play a selection of popular music. Even for all-talk podcasts, music is often part of the program in one form or another. Although music plays an important role in making podcasts sound professional, there are issues around the licensing of musical content within a podcast.

Despite the limitations, there are ways (such as licensing or using Creative Commons licenses) to include music in your podcasts. It's a sticky area, however, and it's important to know the lay of the land before you try to walk across it.

Legalities

Few people may realize this, but each and every time a song is played on the radio, on television, or even at a sporting event, a royalty is paid to the rights holder of that song. How much of a royalty is paid depends on where the song is played. The use of a song in a commercial, such as the Rolling Stones' "Start Me Up" (for Microsoft Windows 2000) or the Beatles' "Revolution" (for a Nike shoe ad), can generate hundreds of thousands or millions of dollars. On the other hand, a radio station playing a particular song might require a payment of only 16 cents. Whatever the cost, royalties are designed to reimburse the creative people who wrote and performed this music.

Many songs are owned not by the artists who wrote them, of course, but by large corporations. Either way, the money is owed fair and square.

As one might expect, podcasting can throw a wrench into the royalty situation when it comes to music. Are the many mom-and-pop operations creating amateur podcasts still responsible for paying royalties for the music they may use in the background during their shows? If the podcast contains licensable music, the answer is YES.

Two main bodies manage royalty collection for music catalogs: ASCAP and BMI. ASCAP (American Society of Composers, Authors and Publishers; **Figure 3.50**) is a performing-arts organization that acts as a collector and advocate for those artists associated with it. BMI (Broadcast Music, Inc.) is similar to ASCAP in that it represents artists with regard to the collection of royalties for music that is played in public. Surprisingly, despite the sudden appearance and rapid growth of podcasting, both of these organizations have agreements that more or less cover the basics for podcasters.

ASCAP has a contract known as the ASCAP Experimental License Agreement for Internet Sites & Services, Release 5.0. This license costs a minimum $288 up front and includes fairly complex fee calculations. This contract is offered on a per-year basis, and the fee is not pro-rated, so if you pay $288 on December 20, 2005, you will have to pay $288 again on January 1, 2006. This is a very dynamic area, however, and any of the above details could change even by the time you read this book. To have a look at ASCAP's license, check out www.ascap.com/weblicense.

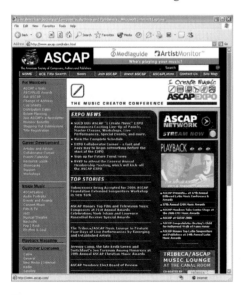

Figure 3.50
ASCAP is the American Society of Composers, Authors and Publishers.

BMI (**Figure 3.51**) has a similar license that appears to be slightly easier to negotiate. The up-front minimum cost of this license is $295, and of course, there are also fee structures, depending on how music is used in the podcasts. To see BMI's license, go to www.bmi.com/licensing/forms/Internet0105A.pdf.

Figure 3.51
BMI's Web site.

note Adobe Acrobat is required to view both of these licenses; you can download it free at www.adobe.com/products/acrobat.

Bob Goyetche, of "The Bob and AJ Show" fame, says that when it comes to playing music in his show, the team ultimately looked at two alternatives:

- "We turned to indie musicians. We get specific permission from songwriters and performers, which gives us permission to play their tunes."

- "The background music we use is Creative Common–licensed music from open-source music sites. Usually, the stipulation is that as long as we give attribution, we can use the material."

It is clear that if you want to create a podcast that includes popular music, and you are interested in proceeding in a legal fashion, you will have to obtain licenses from these organizations and follow the licenses to the letter. That said, it is unclear how many podcasters currently follow these rules. It probably won't surprise anyone if these rules change in the coming months or years. Either way, it is important to stay up to date on this issue if you are an active podcaster.

Creative Commons

Created in 2001 by Lawrence Lessig, Creative Commons (http://creative

Figure 3.52

Creative Commons is an excellent place to find music for your podcasts.

commons.org; **Figure 3.52**) is a not-for-profit organization with the goal of expanding the amount of creative work available for others to build upon and share legally. Creative Commons licenses were originally designed for the United States, but now, Creative Commons licenses can be obtained in 29 countries.

This is a new system, built within current copyright law, that allows an individual to share his or her creations with others and to use music, images, and text online that has been identified as having a Creative Commons license. To learn more about the history of Creative Commons, visit http://creativecommons.org/about/history.

 It's important to note that getting a license with Creative Commons does not mean giving up your copyright. It means instead that you are giving up some of your rights to any taker, but only under certain conditions.

Several of the podcasters I interviewed for this book mentioned Creative Commons as a source for the music they use in their podcasts. If you want to include music in your podcasts, I suggest that you visit the Creative Commons Web site and learn more about what is available. As an artist, you can choose one of several licenses, including:

- *Attribution.* You let others copy, display, perform, and distribute your copyrighted work (and derivative works based upon it), but only if they give you credit.

- *Noncommercial.* You let others copy, display, perform, and distribute your work, but only for noncommercial purposes.

- *No Derivative Works.* You let others copy, display, perform, and distribute only verbatim copies of your work. There can be no derivative works based upon your work.

- *Share Alike.* You allow others to distribute derivative works only under a license that is identical to the license that governs your own work.

The Creative Commons Web site can point you to several excellent sites that contain Creative Commons–licensed sound files and music. One such site is Opsound (www.opsound.com; **Figure 3.53**). This site is an excellent source of music that you can use in your podcasts, provided that you follow the rules of each license. If the idea of reading the license for each song gets under your skin, remember that licensing commercial music is very expensive and requires far more paperwork.

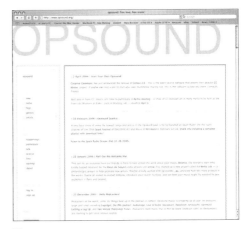

Figure 3.53
Opsound is a great site for Creative Commons–licensed music.

 note Most of the music on the Opsound Web site falls under the Share Alike Creative Commons license, which means you are free to download it, share it, and include it in your work as long as you attribute the works to the original authors/musicians. The site also contains some public-domain music.

Tutorial: Creating a Podcast

Now that I've covered the basic equipment and process of creating a podcast, I'll take you step by step through the process of creating a podcast for both Macintosh and Windows PC computers.

In the case of the Macintosh, I used a third-party microphone, a preamp, and GarageBand in Mac OS X to create the show. On the PC, I used a third-party microphone, no preamp, and Audacity for recording and sound editing.

 On the Macintosh, I used GarageBand as the recording/editing software, and on the Windows PC, I used Audacity. It's important to note that Audacity for the Macintosh behaves and looks almost exactly like its PC counterpart. Therefore, anyone who wants to use Audacity on the Macintosh can refer to the PC tutorial.

I realize that there are literally hundreds of combinations of software, equipment, and operating systems, so I chose two relatively generic setups for creating the podcasts on each platform. The important thing to remember is that the process is fundamentally the same, no matter what is being used to create the show. It goes without saying that a complex preamp/mixing board and a high-end digital recorder will alter the process, but for the purpose of following from idea to finished podcast, these tutorials do the trick.

Creating a Macintosh podcast

 Although other Macintosh programs are available, the fact that GarageBand is bundled with new machines makes it the most ubiquitous sound recording/editing software for the Macintosh. For this reason, I chose to use GarageBand as the software for this tutorial. The list of equipment I used is as follows:

- Karaoke Dynamic Microphone (no joke)

- M-Audio MobilePre USB preamp

- Macintosh G5 dual 2.0 GHz processors, 2.5 GB RAM, Mac OS X 10.3.9

- GarageBand version 3.01

note It's important to note that though I chose to use a preamp to make this podcast, the Mac G5 has a Line-In jack that allows a microphone to be plugged directly into the machine.

1. Connect the equipment

I am assuming that you came up with the concept for the podcast, an outline, and possibly even a script before you made it to this point. That said, the first step is to connect all the equipment properly, starting with connecting the preamp to the USB port and then the microphone to the preamp (**Figures 3.54** through **3.57**). When this is accomplished, ensure that the preamp is receiving power (the lights are on).

Figure 3.54
Connect the preamp to the computer via the USB port.

Figure 3.55
Check to see that the power is active on the preamp.

Figure 3.56
Insert the microphone jack into the preamp microphone input; then set up your microphone with your pop screen (if you have one) in front of you.

Figure 3.57
If you have no preamp, the microphone can be plugged directly into the Line-In jack on the Macintosh.

2. Configure the application and OS

This next step is important, because if the correct inputs aren't selected in System Preferences, the microphone will not work properly. You must also open GarageBand and create a new project for your podcast to be created in. Follow the steps in **Figures 3.58** through **3.66** to set up a straight vocal track (without any effects) so that recording can begin.

Figure 3.58

Open System Preferences, and double-click the Sound icon. Then click the button labeled Input.

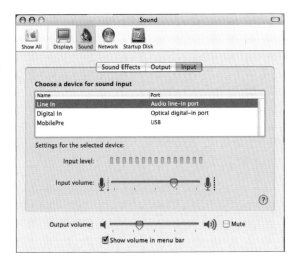

Figure 3.59

In the list box, select MobilePre. (This is the M-Audio MobilePre USB preamp device I am using.)

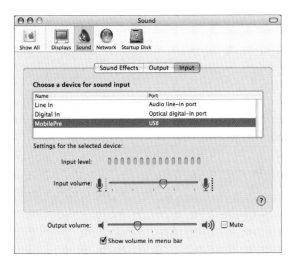

Figure 3.60

Using the microphone, test the Input Level by watching the meter above the volume control. Adjust the volume so that normal speech brings the meter up to about 70 percent of maximum.

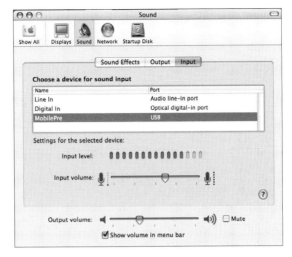

Figure 3.61

Open GarageBand, and if no song is already open, click Create New Song.

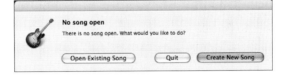

Figure 3.62

When you click Create New Song, you will get this dialog box, asking you what to name it and where to save it. The Tempo, Time, bpm, and Key settings at the bottom of the dialog box can be left as is.

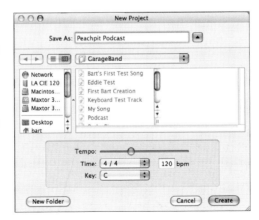

Figure 3.63

When the new GarageBand project opens, you will see a Grand Piano track. Choose Track > Delete Track to delete it.

Figure 3.64

Now choose Track > New Track.

Figure 3.65

In the New Track dialog box, select the Real Instrument radio button and then click Create; this will open the Track Info dialog box, displaying the Real Instrument pane.

Figure 3.66

In the far-left list, select Vocals. The default effect is No Effects; leave this setting as is. For these purposes, Mono is also acceptable (although if you have a stereo microphone, you can click the Stereo button). Click Save Instrument to continue.

tip   If you want to add a digital effect to your voice, you are welcome to do it, but for the first podcast, I suggest that you see what your voice sounds like on its own. If you must use an effect, however, the Male Basic or Female Basic effect is recommended. GarageBand add-on modules, called Jam Packs, are available from Apple for $99 each. They contain elaborate effects that give you more options for editing sound files.

3. Record your podcast

Now that everything is set up and ready to go, it's time to record the podcast. Before you start the actual podcast, record the first couple lines of your podcast; then go back and listen to it (**Figure 3.67**). If you feel that your vocal track needs some adjustment, open the Track Info dialog box by choosing Track > Track Info. Here, you can adjust the equalizer, add effects, and manage echo and reverb.

Figure 3.67
After recording a short test track, if you don't like the sound, you can open the Track Info dialog box (choose Track > Track Info) and make any changes you feel are necessary.

After you have set up your vocals just so, get your script out, and click the Record button to start the podcast (**Figure 3.68** and **Figure 3.69**).

Figure 3.68
Click the Record button, and start talking!

Figure 3.69

If you make a mistake, just pause for a second and then pick up where you left off; the mistake can be edited out later. The other option is to stop the recording and begin a new track.

Play/Pause button

4. Edit your vocal content

The podcast recording is now in the bag. Unfortunately, you made a few verbal flubs and had to repeat yourself in several places to ensure that the material was covered cleanly. This is what editing was made for, and fortunately, it's what GarageBand was made for as well. Using the Track Editor, you can selectively remove (or move around) any portions of the recording that you want (**Figures 3.70** through **3.74**).

Figure 3.70

Begin by selecting the main track (there may be only one); then click the scissor-shaped icon. This brings up the Track Editor, where you can manipulate the recording quickly and easily.

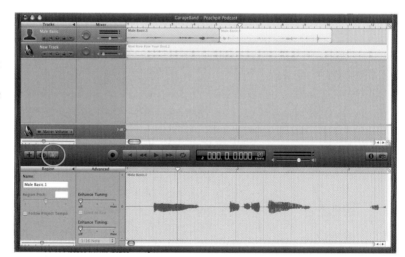

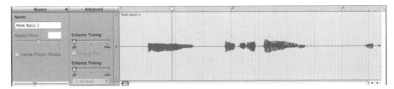

Figure 3.71 In the bottom-left corner of the Track Editor is a slider that allows you to enlarge the scale of the recording strip. Enlarge the scale to between the third and fourth notches.

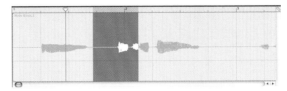

Figure 3.72 Now move to the areas that you want to cut. Using the mouse, select the individual sections of the recording you want to eliminate; then choose Edit > Cut (Command-X).

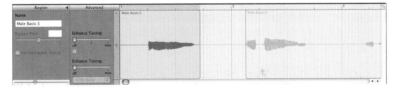

Figure 3.73 When the portion is cut out, there will be a gap in the soundtrack. Use your mouse to grab the far end of the soundtrack and slide the two halves back together again. In this manner, you can remove any unwanted content and join up the recording again so that the listener never knew anything was cut.

Drag the highlighted segment

Figure 3.74

Using the simple cut-and-paste interface in GarageBand, manipulate the recording so that it represents the intended broadcast. This usually involves simple cutting of mistakes and rejoining of the audio track.

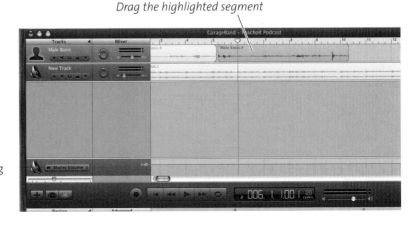

5. Add music and finishing touches

Now is the time to import any music (see "Legalities" earlier in this chapter) into the background and/or at the beginning and end of the podcast. On the Mac, iTunes makes this very simple, because you can drag and drop files directly from iTunes into your podcast (**Figure 3.75**). Similarly, you can drag an MP3 or AAC file from the Desktop into GarageBand.

Figure 3.75

Drag files directly out of iTunes and into GarageBand, if you want. Here, an original version of "Row Row Row Your Boat" is being dragged into GarageBand.

When the music is in place, click the tiny inverted triangle under the track name to open the Track Volume control (**Figure 3.76**). With this control, you can adjust the volume of the track in detail, fading in and out as you please (**Figure 3.77**).

Figure 3.76 When the music is in place, click the inverted triangle to bring up the Track Volume bar. By clicking the volume line in this bar, you create points that you can manipulate to control the volume in minute or heavy-handed ways. Using a series of four points, make your music fade in at the beginning of the podcast and then fade out at the end.

Figure 3.77 Depending on the volume variability of your voice during the recording, you may want to adjust the volume on the main voice track, although I recommend against doing so unless it is absolutely necessary.

6. Export the podcast to MP3 format

The last phase of the podcast-creation process is outputting the file in a usable format. Ideally, the MP3 format is the one that can be accessed by the widest range of listeners, so I recommend that you choose that format. That said, GarageBand does not export in MP3 format; it exports in AAC format into iTunes. For this reason, you must export to iTunes first and then convert to an MP3 file in iTunes to complete the process (**Figures 3.78, 3.79**, and **3.80**).

Figure 3.78

To export your podcast to iTunes, choose Share > Send Song to iTunes.

Figure 3.79

When the export is complete (mixdown is shown here), your podcast will show up in iTunes as the latest file added.

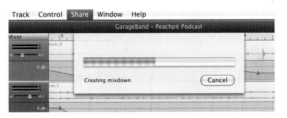

Figure 3.80

In iTunes, select the podcast; then choose Advanced > Convert Selection to AAC to finish the process.

Congratulations—you've completed your first podcast! For instructions on how to publish your podcast, turn to Chapter 5.

Creating a PC podcast

Windows PCs have the largest library of software available for creating podcasts. They also have by far the largest variation in equipment components. PCs have a large variety of motherboards, sound cards, video cards, types of RAM, and even CPUs; for this reason, it is difficult to present an example of a common PC setup for creating podcasts. That said, the vast majority of PCs have sound cards with microphone inputs, and the lion's share of them run the Windows operating system.

I came up with a process for creating a podcast on a PC that a preponderance of PC users will be able to follow, using the following items:

- Radio Shack PZM omnidirectional condenser microphone

- C-Media PCI Sound Card (in Dell Dimension 4500)

- Dell Dimension 4500 P4 2.4 GHz, 1 GB RAM

- Windows XP (although other Windows configurations are very similar)

- Audacity, version 1.2.3 (PC version)

1. Connect the equipment

As in the Macintosh tutorial, I am assuming that you came up with the concept for the podcast, an outline, and possibly even a script before you made it to this point. When you are ready to begin, you must make the necessary connections to get the ball rolling (**Figures 3.81**, **3.82**, and **3.83**). In this case, the connections need only be that the microphone is plugged into the microphone or Line-In jack of the sound card on the back of the PC.

Figure 3.81

In the case of the Realistic (Radio Shack) PZM omnidirectional condenser microphone, check to see that it has a fresh battery (there is no preamp to provide phantom power) before you plug it in.

Figure 3.82

If your microphone has a 6.5mm (1/4-inch) jack, you will likely need an adapter to turn the jack into a standard 3.5mm jack that PC sound cards accept.

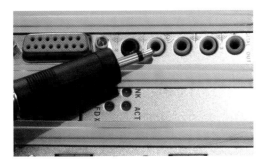

Figure 3.83 Plug the microphone into the microphone input on the sound card (located on the back of your computer). If you make a mistake and plug it into the Line-In jack, it won't be the end of the world; you can always change the input in Audacity later. If you have a pop filter, this is also the time to set it up in front of the microphone.

2. Configure the application and OS

This next step involves making sure that the microphone is working as an input device in Windows. To do this, you must enter the Windows Sounds and Audio Devices control panel and ensure that the microphone is working (**Figures 3.84** through **3.89**).

Figure 3.84

Choose Start > Settings > Control Panel > Sounds, Speech, and Audio Devices.

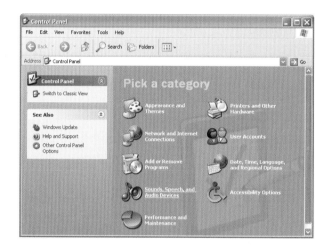

Figure 3.85

Clicking Sounds, Speech, and Audio Devices brings up the Sounds and Audio Devices Properties dialog box. There are five tabs at the top of this dialog box; click the tab labeled Voice.

Figure 3.86

In the Voice Recording area, there is a menu from which you can choose the default recording device. This should already be set to the sound card that is in your computer (in this case, a C-Media card). If you have more than one device available, you can select it here.

Figure 3.87 While still in the Sounds and Audio Devices Properties dialog box, if you want to adjust the balance or the volume of the various inputs to the computer, click the Volume button in the Voice Recording section. This brings up the Recording Control dialog box, which allows you to adjust the volume and balance for four inputs: Microphone, CD Audio, Line In, and Wave.

Figure 3.88

If you want to test that the microphone is working properly, click the Test Hardware button in the Voice Recording section of the Sounds and Audio Devices Properties dialog box. This will bring up the Sound Hardware Test Wizard.

Figure 3.89

After a short time analyzing your system, the wizard shows this dialog box, which allows you to test the functioning of your microphone. When the wizard is complete, the microphone should be working properly.

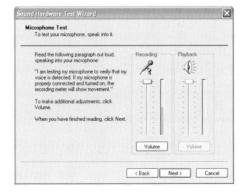

Then you must open Audacity, create a new file, and test your micro-phone to ensure that it is working properly with that program (**Figures 3.90** through **3.93**).

Figure 3.90

Now it's time to launch Audacity. When it's up and running, choose File > Save Project As to name and save your podcast.

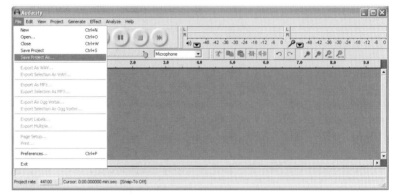

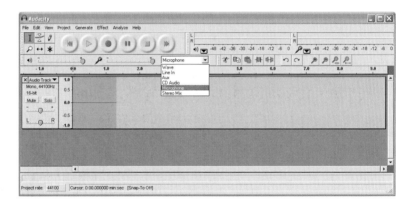

Figure 3.91 In the middle of the main Audacity window is a drop-down menu labeled Microphone. If your microphone is plugged into the microphone jack of your sound card, you're all set. If, however, your microphone is plugged into the Line-In jack, you must select the appropriate input from the Microphone drop-down menu.

Figure 3.92

Next, choose Project >
New Audio Track.

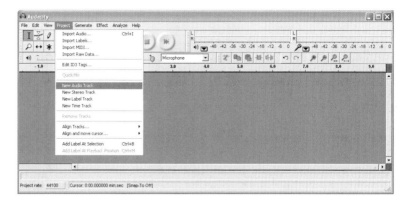

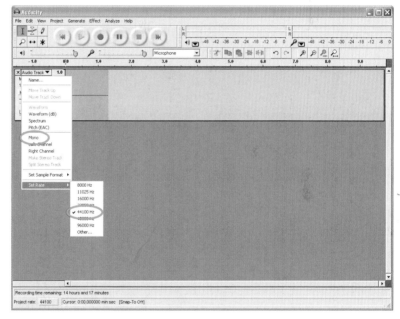

Figure 3.93   The left portion of the Audio Track window will tell you what the recording settings are. These should say Mono and 44100 Hz. If you are using a stereo microphone, you can click the Audio Track control to select a Stereo input. Likewise, if you want to increase or decrease the sampling rate, you can do that in this menu as well. 44100 Hz is 44.1 kHz, which will produce a CD-quality recording.

3. Record your podcast

Now that everything is set up and ready to go, it's time to record the podcast. Before you start the actual podcast, record the first couple lines of your podcast; then go back and listen to it (**Figure 3.94**). If you feel that your vocal track needs some adjustment, and you want to add an effect to it, you can add it *after* the recording (Audacity doesn't add effects dynamically).

Figure 3.94

After recording a short test track, play back the recording to ensure that it sounds OK.

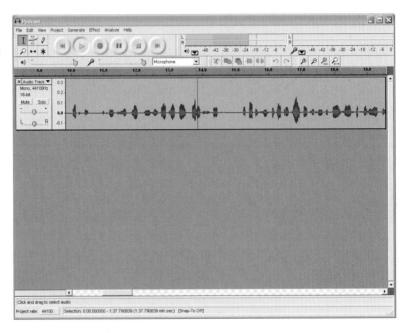

When you have completed the practice run, start the recording, and let it rip (**Figure 3.95** and **Figure 3.96**)!

Figure 3.95
When you're ready,
click the Record button,
and start talking!

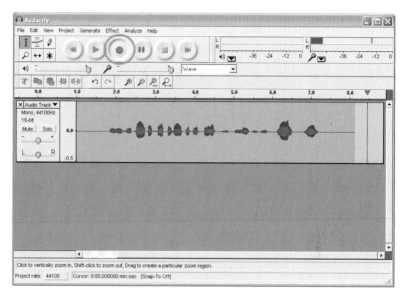

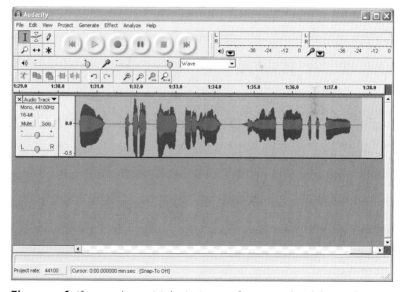

Figure 3.96 If you make a mistake, just pause for a second and then pick up where you left off; the mistake can be edited out later. The other option is to stop the recording and begin a new track. I recommend that you pause and then restart at the point where you made your mistake. This way, you will be editing just one track.

4. Edit your vocal content

The podcast recording is now in the bag. Unfortunately, you made a few verbal flubs and had to repeat yourself in several places to ensure that the material was covered cleanly. This is what editing was made for, and fortunately, the folks who made Audacity have made it easy for us to edit out any verbal mistakes (**Figures 3.97** through **3.100**).

Figure 3.97
Audacity allows you to edit the tracks right in the Audio Track window. To edit a specific portion or add an effect to it, highlight that portion of the track.

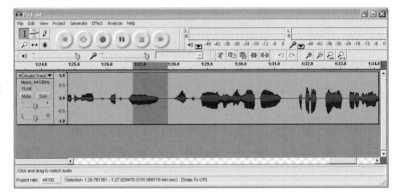

Figure 3.98
When the portion of the track you want to alter is highlighted, click the Effect menu and drag down to the effect you want to apply to the recording. In this case, you are adding an Echo effect to the selection.

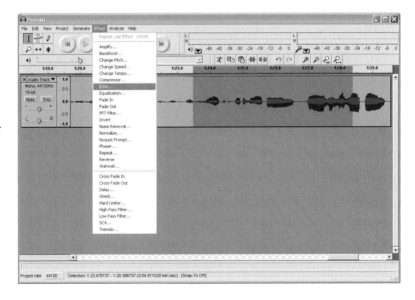

Figure 3.99

If you want to remove a specific portion, select that portion; then choose Edit > Cut. When you do this, the portion you selected will be cut from the recording.

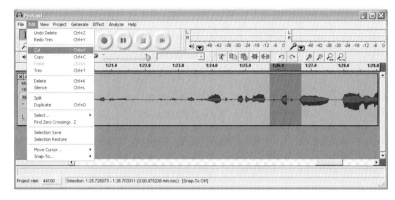

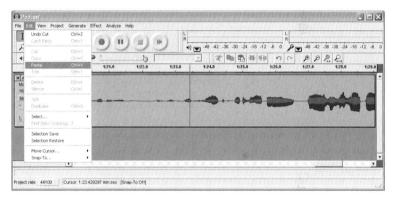

Figure 3.100 To move a portion of the recording around, choose Edit > Cut. Then, using the selection tool, click the place in the recording where you want the cut piece of audio to be placed. When the area is selected (a line will appear in the recording showing the exact point of insertion), choose Edit > Paste.

5. Add music and finishing touches

The voice recording is now just right, but it's just a plain voice recording. Now is the time to import any music (see "Legalities" earlier in this chapter) into the background and/or at the beginning and end of the podcast. Audacity allows for the easy drag-and-drop addition of any MP3 or WAV file. Simply pick up the MP3 file you want, and drag it to the area beneath your main sound track (**Figure 3.101**). The MP3 will be added as a separate audio track.

Figure 3.101

Drag audio files directly to Audacity. When you do, the files will be imported automatically.

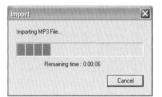

When the music is in place, you can highlight specific sections and adjust the volume or apply effects such as a fade-in or fade-out as you see fit (**Figures 3.102, 3.103**, and **3.104**).

Figure 3.102

When the music is in place, you can adjust the volume control on the bar on the left, or you can select portions of the music and add effects to it. This is where you can add the Fade In and Fade Out effects.

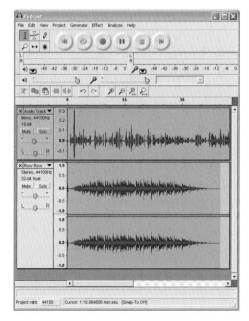

Figure 3.103

Note the (very loud) MP3 recording and how it is tapered at both ends. This file has had a short Fade In and a longer Fade Out effect added to it.

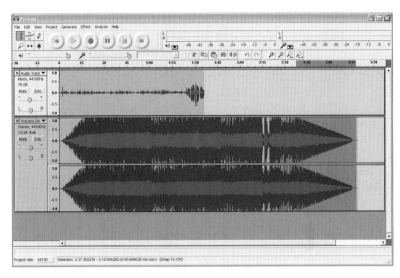

Figure 3.104

If you want to add any effects to any portion of the recording, now is the time to do it. To add an effect, simply select the portion of the recording that you want to alter; then choose the effect you want to add from the Effect menu. You can undo the addition of effects, if need be.

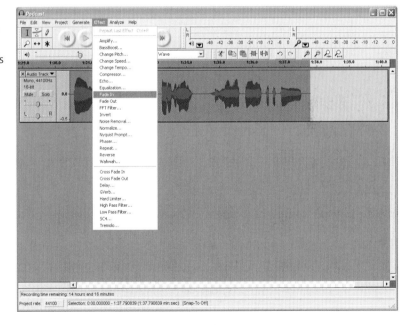

6. Export the podcast to MP3 format

The last phase of the podcast-creation process is outputting the file in a usable format. Ideally, the MP3 format is the one that can be accessed by the widest range of listeners, so I recommend that you choose that format (**Figures 3.105**, **3.106**, and **3.107**). Audacity can export files as WAV files, MP3 files, or Ogg Vorbis files. For purposes of mass acceptance, the MP3 is the file of choice.

Figure 3.105
When the podcast is complete, choose File > Export As MP3.

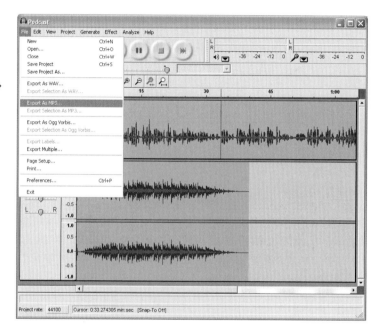

Figure 3.106 When you select Export As MP3 file, a warning appears that the file will be mixed down into two tracks (a stereo recording). This is fine.

Figure 3.107

Next, a dialog box asks you to name the file and select a place to save it. This dialog box also allows you to change your mind about what kind of file format to save it in. That's it! When the file has been exported as an MP3 file, the job is complete.

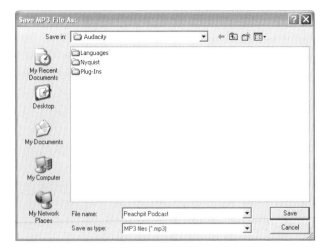

Creating Podcasts from Commercial Sources

Although I mentioned this topic in Chapter 2, I'll quickly touch on the process for creating podcasts from commercial material. The commercial sources in this case are radio shows, television shows, periodicals, and audiobooks that are available over the Internet or from devices such as the Griffin radio SHARK or software like Replay Radio. I also need to note that these are personal podcasts—made or purchased specifically for your own enjoyment. They are not meant to be shared with others.

The process of creating a personal podcast is as simple as downloading the file from a Web site or using a device like the Griffin radio SHARK to capture a radio show locally and turn it into an MP3 or AAC file for your iPod (or other MP3 player). Commercial Web sites like Audible.com offer audiobooks, newspapers, and magazines in podcast (audio) form, and obtaining them requires only that you pay (with a credit card) for the content.

Many radio stations are now creating podcasts with their content, including public radio systems like NPR (United States), CBC (Canada), BBC (United Kingdom), and ABC (Australia). These podcast files are available for the taking from the respective Web sites. Also, Replay Radio can troll the Internet airwaves (many of the world's terrestrial radio stations also broadcast over the Internet) and record any program you want. When they're recorded, you can easily download these files to your MP3 player or iPod for enjoyment wherever you go. Also note that many media Web sites—ABC News, ESPN, TSN, and the like—all have podcast sections, with a fair portion of their content available in this format.

4

Video Podcasting

This chapter covers the basics of video podcasting, also known as video blogging (vlogging) and vodcasting. Video podcasting has jumped onto the podcasting map almost as quickly as podcasting jumped onto the map of broadcasters everywhere. This chapter takes a look at video podcasting and its effect on podcasting in general. Then it shows you how to put together the video portion of a podcast, from important production concepts, to the equipment needed, to recording and editing the video portion of the podcast on both the Mac and PC.

Defining Video Podcasting

When the first edition of *Secrets of Podcasting: Audio Blogging for the Masses* first appeared on the shelves, it covered the heart and soul of podcasting, which at the time was audio-based podcasting. Sure, video blogging had been around for some time, but the vast majority of podcasting revolved around the audio version. Probably the biggest reason was that at the time, there really weren't any mainstream portable video players that allowed users to watch podcasts away from their computers. In fact, the computer was pretty much the only viable device on which to view video podcasts, and though many people enjoy watching podcasts on their computers, a huge part of the appeal of podcasting is that it's a very mobile medium that allows you to enjoy podcasts nearly anywhere.

In October 2005, Apple released its new iPod, which users immediately dubbed the video iPod. Featuring a 30 GB or 60 GB hard drive and a crisp 2.5-inch color screen, the new iPod could play movies; music videos; television shows; home movies; and, yes, even video podcasts right in the palm of the user's hand. This single product announcement took video blogging from a small niche that a few people explored with their computers to a legitimate segment of the growing podcasting realm.

 Certainly, a few compact digital media players could handle video content before Apple jumped into the fray with its video iPod, but like it or not, Apple's role in the world of digital music, digital media players, and podcasting is a significant one. Therefore, I am not ignoring the other players on the market; I'm just sticking to the events that propelled video podcasting into the mainstream.

Video podcasting has quickly taken a share of the podcasting market, with content that ranges from network television shows to mom-and-pop vodcasts created in dingy basements. How video podcasting will continue to evolve is anyone's guess, but in a few short months, it has caused plenty of ripples in broadcast media circles.

Vlogs

As I mentioned earlier in this book, *blog* is a term that derives from the words that describe it: *Web log*. *Web log* became *blog,* and in much the same way, *video Web logs* became *vlogs*. Vlogs are really the precursors of video podcasts, although vlogging per se never really took off and reached a large audience.

Video blogs first appeared around 2000, but they didn't start to find purchase in the fertile soil of the World Wide Web until 2004, when programs like Transistr (formerly known as iPodderX) offered video podcatching features. When the fifth-generation video iPod hit the market, and the iTunes Music Store started selling television shows and music videos for it, video podcasting really began to take off. Now the number of video podcasts available in the directories grows daily, and popular video podcasts like "Tiki Bar TV" (**Figure 4.1**) are finding an audience as the evolved form of video blogs.

Figure 4.1

"Tiki Bar TV" is a popular video podcast.

Exploring Video Podcasts

Although a video podcast is pretty much a video podcast, I have a classification system that I like to group video podcasts into. This system isn't scientific; it's just what makes the most sense to me, and it has some value because the content of video podcasts can vary greatly from category to category.

Homemade vodcasts

The first—and some people would say the purest—form of video podcasts is homemade video podcasts, created by amateurs who are interested in covering some topic that interests them personally. These programs are basically the same as audio podcasts, but they have a visual element, often not much different from that of a "talking head" news program.

Four great examples of homemade video podcasts:

- "Rocketboom"
- "Rumor Girls" (**Figure 4.2**)
- "Hockey Strike Webcom"
- "Mobility Today Video Podcast"

Figure 4.2

The "Rumor Girls" Web site.

Video-aficionado vodcasts

Video podcasts in the second category are commercial-quality video podcasts. These may also be created by aficionados of a particular topic, but these folks are technically savvy and/or have access to high-quality video equipment and editing software, which makes the quality of their podcasts superior. A few good examples:

- "Happy Tree Friends"

- "Tiki Bar TV"

- "Beach Walks with Rox"

- "Cooking Kitty Corner" (**Figure 4.3**)

Figure 4.3

The "Cooking Kitty Corner" Web site.

Commercial-outreach vodcasts

Vodcasts in this category are created to extend the reach of commercial enterprises. These include video podcasts like the following:

- "Barenaked Ladies Podcast" (**Figure 4.4**)

- "The Ricky Gervais Podcast"

- "PC Gamer Podcast"

Figure 4.4

BNL Blog, the Web home of "Barenaked Ladies Podcast."

Converted-media vodcasts

The fourth podcast category includes the pure commercial podcasts that are derived straight from other forms of media: television shows and music videos that are available through the iTunes Music Store, as well as other television shows that are redirected into podcasts free of charge.

Although the quality of video podcasts generally goes up the closer one moves toward a commercial source, there are always exceptions to the rule. There certainly are some very high-quality homemade vodcasts, and there are also some poorly made commercial podcasts. That said, the general rule still applies.

Top Ten Video Podcasts

During the writing of this book, the top ten video podcasts, according to Podcast Alley (**Figure 4.5**), are

1. "GeekBrief.TV" (http://geekbrief.podshow.com)

2. "Port City P.D." (www.portcitypd.com)

3. "Izzy Video" (www.channelfrederator.com)

4. "Channel Frederator" (www.channelfrederator.com)

5. "Tiki Bar TV" (http://tikibartv.blogspot.com)

6. "Rumor Girls" (www.rumorgirls.com)

7. "Rocketboom" (www.rocketboom.com/vlog)

8. "Icenrye's Geocaching Videozine" (www.icenrye.com/newsite)

9. "PhotoWalkthrough.com" (www.photowalkthrough.com)

10. "ScreenCastsOnline" (http://screencastsonline.com/sco)

Figure 4.5
Podcast Alley's list of top video podcasts at www.podcastalley.com.

Watching Video Podcasts

As mentioned earlier in this chapter, the release of Apple's video iPod is what really sparked the video podcasting boom, but several other quality handheld digital media players handle video spectacularly. It's also important not to forget that hunk of plastic, wires, and blinking lights that's sitting on your desk; after all, your computer is perhaps the best way of all to view video podcasts.

This section takes a quick look at the top few handheld players for video podcasting, as well as a few of the computer programs that are useful for viewing them. For detailed specs on the players, see Chapter 2.

Apple video iPod

The video iPods are fantastic little machines, and despite their small screens, they are surprisingly functional. As of this writing, Apple has only two video iPods available, but there are rumors that a new widescreen video iPod is in the works. No doubt a widescreen iPod would push vodcasting even farther toward the mainstream.

Photo courtesy of Apple Computer, Inc

The screen on the iPod is a QVGA 320x240 2.5-inch color screen, which makes navigating the menus a treat.

Archos Gmini 500

win

The Archos is a high-end portable video, audio, photo, and music player with a stunning 4-inch color screen. The price reflects the high-end nature of this device, but when video podcasting enters the equation, having a larger and brighter screen is important.

If a high-end, all-in-one video device is what you're looking for, the Gmini must be considered for its large, crisp color screen, if for no other reason. The addition of plenty of useful features makes it a worthy option, although a very pricey one.

Placing Movies on Your iPod

 Although it is not legal in the United States to copy commercial DVDs, even for your own use, software is available that allows you to rip DVDs to an iPod for viewing. In fact, you can put as many as 75 full-length movies on a 60 GB video iPod. I do not recommend or even suggest that you copy commercial DVDs in this way, but if you have a large library of home movies on DVD (perhaps created by iMovie), software like HandBrake (**Figure 4.6**) for the Macintosh and/or Windows can turn those home movies into mini-movies that you can watch on your iPod.

Figure 4.6

HandBrake is an excellent tool for putting home movies on your iPod.

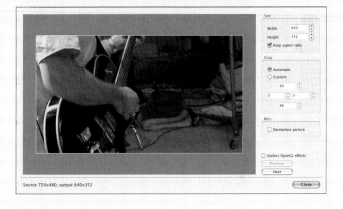

iRiver U10

 When it comes to viewing video, the U10 is heavily limited by its 1 GB of storage space. That said, a stripped-down, full-length home-movie DVD (that is, one that's made to look good on a 2.2-inch screen) usually comes in at around 600 MB, so it *is* possible to store a reasonable amount of video content on the U10. The difference between the U10 and the Creative or Apple players is that of a single movie-length video versus 50 or 60 movie-length videos.

When you're shopping for a Windows-based digital music device, you cannot ignore the iRiver U10. The inclusion of an FM radio and a built-in voice recorder automatically save money compared with Apple's iPods, for which those features are available only as add-ons. That said, the U10 has very limited storage space: only 1 GB.

iTunes

As mentioned earlier in this book, iTunes is not just a reservoir for your music; it's also an access point to the iTunes Music Store and a receptacle for videos, home movies, and podcasts. iTunes has a built-in media player, making vodcasting just another portion of the system. Double-clicking a vodcast in the library causes it to start playing in a small window inside the iTunes window (**Figure 4.7**); another double-click on the window brings it up to full screen. Whether you use a Mac or a Windows PC, iTunes is an excellent tool for viewing video podcasts.

Figure 4.7

iTunes on the Mac.

Windows Media Player

Windows Media Player (**Figure 4.8**) is a ubiquitous media player that can play video podcasts with ease on either Macintosh or Windows computers, although WMP is used predominantly on Windows machines. Video podcasts typically are in MP4 format, and as such, they are playable in WMP 10 (the most recent version).

Figure 4.8

Windows Media Player 10 in action.

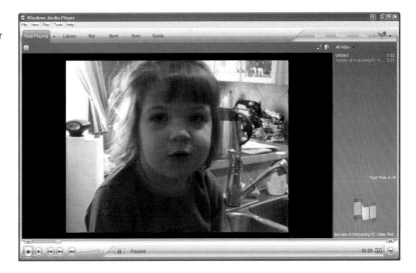

Zen Vision:M

Creative's Zen Vision:M can store 120 hours of movies, television shows, music videos, video podcasts, and video content in general. Some people feel that the screen on the Zen Vision:M is superior to that on Apple's video iPod, and I have to say that I agree with them. For video podcasts, the Zen Vision:M is a particularly solid choice and one that you should consider if watching vodcasts is your main goal.

Creating a Video Podcast

Creating a video podcast can be a dramatically different process from creating an audio podcast, or it can be fairly similar. It all depends on what kind of video podcast you are creating. If the vodcast contains how-to videos that don't require audio, the podcast can be created much like an audio podcast, with the audio portion simply laid over the video portion. Most video podcasts, however, involve more complex video work, with scripts, lighting, and all the usual audio issues that go along with audio podcasting. This section takes a look at the intricacies of video podcasting, including a walkthrough of editing video content on Adobe Premiere on Windows and iMovie on the Macintosh.

Several factors are important when you are getting ready to create a video podcast. The equipment is critically important, as are the lighting, the script, the on-air talent, the background or set, and the software used to edit and create the vodcast. The key elements that I examine here are equipment, software, lighting, script, and audio.

Video cameras

Obviously, the most important piece of equipment in creating a video podcast is the video recorder. Like nearly everything else in the world of technology, video cameras come in a wide range of quality levels and prices, and it's important to note that a high price does not always mean quality. The number of video cameras on the market is truly staggering, so as usual, I endeavor to cover three recommended cameras: budget, midrange, and professional.

IEEE 1394

An *IEEE 1394* (pronounced "eye-triple-E-thirteen-ninety-four") is a device that allows the easy connection of the camcorder and a computer equipped with a FireWire port. The bonus of this is that the digital video can stream directly from the camcorder into the computer in digital form without having to go through a converter. If you can avoid converting from analog, by all means do so.

Canon ZR100

The Canon ZR100 (**Figure 4.9**) is the budget model that I'm recommending. At $299.95, it's a very inexpensive DV camcorder that still offers decent picture quality and ease of use, with an iEEE 1394 connector for hooking up to your computer. The ZR100 uses MiniDV tapes and can record up to 120 minutes in long-play mode (although this mode decreases quality).

Figure 4.9

The Canon ZR100.

The ZR100 offers some nice features for a low-budget model, including:

- 16:9 widescreen picture

- Low-light video setting

- Built-in effects

- Built-in microphone

- PCM digital sound

- 2.4-inch TFT color display

Sony DCR-HC96 Handycam

Sony has a long history of making quality camcorders, and the DCR-HC96 MiniDV Handycam (**Figure 4.10**) is no exception to this rule.

Figure 4.10

The Sony DCR-HC96 Handycam.

At $799.99, the DCR-HC96 falls in the midrange of cameras, but it also sports higher quality and some nicer features for budding video podcasters. For one thing, it comes with a built-in camera feature (via a memory stick) that allows you to take quality still pictures with the camera as well as video. One of the bonuses of the DCR-HC96 is the included analog-to-digital pass-through converter, which allows you to run in an analog signal (like from an old camcorder or from a VCR) and pass it through the camcorder to digitize it. Devices that do just that cost as much as $199 alone.

The feature set of the DCR-HC96 is a long list, but the highlights include

- 3.3-megapixel CCD imager

- 10x optical zoom

- Carl Zeiss lens

- Analog-to-digital conversion with pass-through

- Digital effects

- USB connectivity

- Fader effects

- i.LINK DV interface

- Manual focus

- Onscreen controls

- Infrared night-shot capability

It's worth noting that some of the long-standing Sony features, such as SteadyShot and the Tele Macro function, are well worth having. If you can afford it, I recommend getting a camcorder of this type.

Panasonic AG-HVX200

For those who are really serious about vodcasting, I recommend going with the professional-level, highly touted Panasonic AG-HVX200

Figure 4.11
The high-end camcorder, this Panasonic can create HD video.

(**Figure 4.11**). At $5,995, this is not an inexpensive camera, but the quality and feature set make it worth all that extra money. If you are serious about video podcasting, and you plan to be doing it for years to come, I suggest investing your hard-earned savings in a high-quality camera like this one.

The most striking and important difference about this camera is that it's a true high-definition camera, allowing for HD recording formats such as 1080i and 720p. You can also control the frame rates with ease, giving you a huge amount of control over the quality of the video shot.

The feature list of the HVX 200 is as follows:

- High Definition image quality with low compression

- Multiple recording formats

- High-resolution 3.5-inch display

- Manual zoom

- Two P2 card slots that can be hot-swapped

- MiniDV tape transport for DV recording

- 48 kHz, 16-bit, 4-channel digital PCM audio

Converting Analog Video

  Let's say that you want to be a vodcaster, but all you have is an old analog camcorder, and you don't have $800 to spend on new equipment. The obvious problem becomes how you are going to get the analog video signal into your decidedly digital computer.

Several handy products can solve this problem, but none of them is as efficient and high quality as the Data Video DAC-100 DV converter (**Figure 4.12**). This device takes analog video signals from such devices as analog video recorders or VCRs (or even television signals, for that matter) and converts them to digital signals that your computer can understand. At $199, it's not super inexpensive, but it's a far cry from $800 for a DV camcorder with an analog pass-through!

Figure 4.12
The DAC-100 converts analog video signals to the digital signals your computer can understand.

Microphones

Most camcorders come with built-in microphones. Several problems, however, are inherent with built-in microphones, not the least of which is the fact that the cameraman is much closer to the microphone than the subject of the video is. Therefore, if the cameraman clears his or her throat, the resulting noise is audible on the video tape.

Fortunately, most camcorders have a microphone jack that enables you to connect your own external microphone. Plenty of microphones can be plugged into a camcorder, so you can pretty much take your pick. One decent option is Griffin Technology's LapelMic (see Chapter 3), but any portable lapel microphone will do.

 note Don't use the built-in microphone on the camcorder unless you have absolutely no other choice; the sound quality is always distant and unprofessional. Always use a clip-on microphone that the subject of the video can wear or a handheld microphone that the subject can cling to as he or she speaks.

Tripods

Although many people like to create a "modern" video by implementing a shaky handheld look, for those of us over the age of 30, that technique gets old quickly. I recommend that for most of your video podcasting work, you use a video tripod like the Bogen/Manfrotto video tripod (**Figure 4.13**). The steady, calm video that a tripod affords is well worth the extra cost. Technically, any tripod can do the job, but video tripods have a little arm that allows you to move the camera with the arm rather than grab the camera itself.

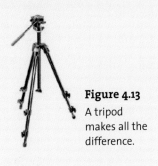

Figure 4.13
A tripod makes all the difference.

Lighting

When it comes to video recording, lighting is one of the most important factors. Let's face it—improper lighting makes finished video look flat, dull, and unappealing, whereas proper lighting is so natural that it goes completely unnoticed. I can impart on you a few truisms and tips for successful lighting:

- Avoid direct sunlight, if possible; it tends to overexpose parts of the video frame and can cause your subjects to squint.

- Chris Breen from Playlist (www.playlistmag.com) recommends shooting outside only on overcast days, because the light on overcast days is more diffuse and even.

- If you are shooting a "talking heads" type of vodcast, try to shoot in the same place or a series of similar places every time so that the quality and exposure are consistent from vodcast to vodcast.

- Try to avoid any conditions in which the lighting is apt to change quickly. That goes for both indoor and outdoor shoots.

Script/plan

Just like with the audio podcast, I can't stress enough that the best plan is to have a plan. Take the time to write a script so that you have something to follow during the show. If the show is conversational in nature, have a list of topics to keep the conversation flowing. If it's an interview show, have your list of questions at the ready. If, however, it's a "talking head" news show, a script becomes increasingly essential unless you are that rare breed of person who can wing it without any structure.

Software

A large number of possibilities is available when it comes to video editing for the Mac and PC. I'm going to stick to a pair of programs for each platform, each of which is a proven, solid performer with which you really can't go wrong. That said, with the plethora of video editing programs out there (many of which come with a new computer or

Interview with Ben Williams of "Digital Media Tips N Tricks"

Ben Williams is the vodcaster of "Digital Media Tips N Tricks" (www.codedsignal.com/serendipity; **Figure 4.14**). He is also New York City digital-media specialist at J Walter Thompson.

Figure 4.14
Ben Williams walking the beat.

Farkas: What got you interested in podcasting?

Williams: I am passionate about technology, but I tend to go for what is functional—geeky yet practical. Podcasting was a natural progression for me, due to my video and Web background, and I've been waiting for this moment over 7 years.

I kept seeing articles in magazines on podcasting back in March 2005. I began to download and listen to podcasts like "Engadget," "The Point," "The Web Hosting Show," and "Media Artist Secrets," I was in tech-geek heaven. I started to think, "Wow—maybe we can use this new method to send files to our clients." Upon my exploration of the medium, I realized that there were possibilities that go far beyond file sharing. I guess August 2005 is when I totally got hooked.

Farkas: What was the genesis of your podcast?

Williams: "Digital Media Tips N Tricks" was my first show. I thought, "Digital media is not only my job; it's a hobby." Initially, I wanted to build up an online community and discuss various digital-media standards, tips, and tricks. I realized early on that I did not have time to manage a community; I wanted to podcast and focus on the content.

"Beneath the Beat" (**Figure 4.15**) is my second show. It is focused on the authentic culture of hip-hop. Originally, my partner Logan was going to take control of the show while I handled "Digital Media Tips N Tricks." We had discussed how we wanted it to be a talk show examining the various elements and people in the hip-hop culture. There were a number of unforeseen events that prevented that from happening.

Figure 4.15
The "Beneath the Beat" Web site.

Interview with Ben Williams of "Digital Media Tips N Tricks" (continued)

Farkas: What is your opinion about the commercialization of podcasting?

Williams: For over a century, ad agencies and media networks have been highly effective in using programming to shape uniform consumer buying habits. But digital technology has changed the terrain. There is a dilemma in trying to merge traditional strategies with podcasting. In most cases, the 30-second commercial will not apply here. The advertisers need to realize this and adapt to the medium. Once intrusive marketing models are adopted, the author stands to lose credibility, and core audience perception can alter brand equity.

I have spoken to and interviewed both podcasters and the listeners on this very subject. Many of the people listening to podcasts left television and radio because they were fed up with the programming; however, people are comfortable with putting up with advertising if it's minimal and relevant to the podcast.

Here's a good example: A mother is raising a toddler and is expecting another baby any day now. She regularly listens to a podcast titled "Healthy Parenting." At the beginning and midway through the program, the host of the show takes 8 to 15 seconds to introduce the sponsor, a diaper company called Pick Me Ups: "Pick Me Ups, the diaper for the big kid in you. Go to www.pickmeups.com."

The simplicity of the ad will not only work in this market, but if the podcaster happens to work in how it helped him or her with potty training the little ones, and later goes on to discuss the psychological benefits and experiences of that child, it's a no-brainer; it will sell. People are into what's practical, and they tend to go off word-of-mouth recommendations, especially from someone they regard and spend time with.

Farkas: When did it occur to you that video podcasting was the way to go, rather than the audio format?

Williams: Both audio and video have their place. Some specialized programs are just best left as audio only. The obvious benefit to audio podcasts is that people use them while working out, en route to and from work, or we can talk about the people who connect their device to their car as a stereo replacement. I still think there are going to be varied uses for audio, but video will likely command a much larger audience in the long run.

with a video-card purchase), you are more than welcome to use software that you already own and are familiar with. For the most part, these programs are not all that different to begin with.

Adobe Premiere Elements 2.0

Adobe makes what is arguably the best of the Windows-based video editing packages: Adobe Premiere Pro. At $899, Premiere Pro is certainly for high-end video enthusiasts. But those of us who are budget conscious need not worry, because Adobe has a $99 version of Premiere known as Premiere Elements 2.0 (**Figure 4.16**), and it's a fantastic and powerful package for the money! If you aren't convinced, you can download a 30-day free trial from www.adobe.com.

Figure 4.16

Premiere Elements 2.0 is an outstanding piece of software for the price.

Premiere Elements 2.0 offers these features:

- Can transfer DV footage via FireWire or USB 2.0

- Custom editing studio

- Hundreds of special effects to customize your footage

- Can preview effects before they are applied to video segments

- Hundreds of unique transitions

- Can create DVD menus and burn DVDs directly

All but true video professionals can get by with the feature set that Elements 2.0 provides. If video podcasting is something that you are going to be doing weekly, a more powerful program might be warranted, but you can certainly get by with Elements 2.0 without worrying that the audience will notice.

Final Cut Express HD

Like Adobe, Apple offers a boiled-down version of its famous video editing program, Final Cut Pro 5, which retails for $1,299. At $299, Final Cut Express HD (**Figure 4.17**) isn't as inexpensive as Adobe's lower-level offering, but it is decidedly more powerful.

Figure 4.17
Final Cut Express HD packs a lot of power for only $299.

Final Cut Express HD is a very powerful cut-down version of the Final Cut Pro software, which has been used to edit many Hollywood movies, such as *Cold Mountain*. At first glance, Final Cut Express HD looks very much like its more expensive sibling, and not surprisingly, it has many high-end features that are bound to make even hard-core video aficionados drool.

Final Cut Express HD offers these features:

- Can edit DV and HDV projects

- Soundtrack (custom music-creation software) included in the package

- Can integrate multilayer Adobe Photoshop files

- Allows creation and synchronization of voice-overs

- Advance color correction on the fly

- Includes Live Type, which creates dynamic text and graphics that can be animated right in the project

- Hundreds of professional transitions and digital effects

- Seamless import of iMovie files

Of all the software I talk about in this section, Final Cut Express HD is the most powerful by far. For those who want extreme power, Final Cut Pro 5 is the right choice for Mac users, and Adobe Premiere Pro is the correct selection for Windows users. For the Mac user who wants the ability to start simply and expand later, Final Cut Express HD is the better choice. You can start with iMovie (which comes with every new Macintosh), and when you are ready to move up to more power, you can simply import the iMovie files directly into Final Cut Express HD to take them to the next level.

iMovie HD 6

iMovie HD 6 (**Figure 4.18**) is the bundled video editing software that comes with all new Macintosh computers. It's also available as part of the iLife '06 software package for $99.

Figure 4.18

iMovie HD 6 is a powerful yet inexpensive tool for video editing. Shown here is a transition between scenes.

iMovie Add-Ons

iMovie has plenty of great digital effects built right into it, but it's great to know that an entire third-party industry supplies a host of very cool plug-ins for everything from transitions to audio tools and onscreen graphics. One great source of these products is GeeThree (www.geethree.com; **Figure 4.19**), which makes a series of plug-ins titled Slick effects.

Figure 4.19

GeeThree is a great source of add-ons for iMovie.

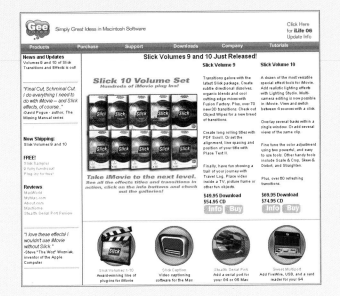

Another company that offers some exciting plug-ins is eZedia (www.ezedia.com). eZedia offers several tools (as well as plug-ins) for iMovie that allow you to do image tilting, rotating, and even layering.

Stupendous Software (www.stupendous-software.com) also offers an interesting set of iMovie plug-ins that add cool effects and functionality to the program.

So many plug-ins are available that I could write an entire chapter about them. My suggestion is that if you're using iMovie, and you're looking for ways to stretch iMovie further and get more out of it, have a look at the many companies that offer plug-ins that allow you to do some cool stuff for free!

iMovie is an important piece of software because it brought high-level video editing to the mainstream. When iMovie hit the streets, average people could all of a sudden take their home movies and turn them into something special with digital effects, menus, credits, and spectacular scene transitions, all with a few clicks of the mouse. iMovie's success inspired other software makers to create similar programs, and the result has been somewhat of a revolution in video editing on the home computer.

The beauty of iMovie lies in its interface and fundamental simplicity. Every aspect of using iMovie is a breeze. From importing video files to editing them, to adding visual effects and transitions, all parts of iMovie are simple and intuitive.

The feature set for iMovie includes

- Predesigned themes

- Real-time digital effects

- Cinematic real-time titling

- Enhanced audio tools and audio effects

- GarageBand scoring

- Integration with iDVD

- Easy video podcast publishing via iWeb

For Macintosh users, iMovie HD 6 (or even older versions of iMovie) is a great way to whet an appetite for video podcasting. Indeed, iMovie is powerful enough that you need never move up to any other piece of software. Because iMovie comes with every new Macintosh and is also available in iLife '06 for a mere $99, iMovie is the best choice for most beginning Macintosh podcasters.

Movie Maker 2

It can be argued that Movie Maker was Microsoft's direct answer to Apple's inclusion of iMovie with its computers. Whatever the case, it doesn't really matter, because Movie Maker 2 (the current version) is an easy-to-use piece of software that allows Windows users to import, edit, and export digital video in an easy-to-use environment. For those who are familiar with iMovie, Movie Maker 2 (**Figure 4.20**) likely won't live up to their expectations, but this software is outstanding in its own right and gives first-time vodcasters a free tool with which to create their video masterpieces.

Figure 4.20

Movie Maker 2 is the Windows equivalent of iMovie for the Mac.

Movie Maker 2 has everything you need to create basic yet professional-looking video podcasts:

- Can import analog (with additional adapter) or digital video

- Creates transitions between clips

- Incorporates slides, background music, sound effects, and voice-overs

- 28 digital effects

- Audio effects/editing available

Ultimately, Movie Maker 2 isn't as robust as iMovie is, but that doesn't mean that it's not a worthwhile piece of software for beginning vodcasters. In fact, the price (free/included with Windows XP) can't be beat, and if you have an older version of Movie Maker, you can truck on over to www.microsoft.com and download the newest version gratis.

Microsoft's Web site also offers detailed tutorials on Movie Maker 2.

Creating a Video Podcast on a Windows PC

win

Because the audio portions of podcast creation are covered in detail in Chapter 3, I don't rehash those aspects here. Indeed, these tutorials are meant to show you how to import, edit, and convert video to a video podcast that you can then publish (see Chapter 5) however you see fit.

For this tutorial, I'm using Movie Maker 2 because it is available with Windows XP and is also available for free download from Microsoft's Web site. The following steps show you exactly how to get the video from your digital camcorder onto your computer, and then edit and manipulate the video to make it look as good as possible. Last, I show you how to tweak the audio portion of the vodcast and export it in a format that can be viewed by podcast watchers everywhere.

1. Connect the equipment

To connect a digital video camera to a computer, you need either of two connectors: a USB 2.0 connector or an IEEE 1394 FireWire connector. Both of these connectors are high-bandwidth connections, meaning that they can handle the large amount of information that must stream from the camcorder into the computer. An old-fashioned USB 1.1 connector simply isn't fast enough, so you must have either USB 2.0 or FireWire. In this case, I'm using a FireWire connection from my Sony digital Handycam (**Figure 4.21**) to my custom-made Athlon-powered PC with a FireWire jack right on the front (**Figure 4.22**).

Figure 4.21

A Sony digital camcorder (in this case, a DCR-TRV350).

Figure 4.22
My PC has a FireWire jack on the front. Many computers now do.

To connect the camcorder and the computer, you need the correct cable, which can be purchased separately but often comes with the camcorder. In this case, it's an IEEE 1394 cable (**Figure 4.23**) Start by connecting one end of the cable to the camcorder (**Figure 4.24**) and the other end to the computer (**Figure 4.25**).

Figure 4.23
An IEEE 1394 cable.

Figure 4.24
Connect the IEEE 1394 cable to the camcorder.

Figure 4.25
Connect the other end of the IEEE 1394 cable to the computer.

2. Start the software and turn on the camcorder

Next, you need to open Movie Maker 2 (**Figure 4.26**) and power up your camcorder into VCR mode (**Figure 4.27**). Doing this allows Movie Maker to control your camcorder directly, which means that you can forget about fumbling with the camcorder's controls and can just stick with the controls in Movie Maker 2.

Figure 4.26

Open Movie Maker 2.

Figure 4.27

Set your camcorder to VCR mode.

3. Import the video into Movie Maker

When Movie Maker 2 is open and the camcorder is connected, the program immediately senses the camcorder, and the connection happens automatically. When this occurs, you immediately face the Video Capture Wizard (**Figure 4.28**), where you enter the name of the video and pick the location where it is to be saved on the hard drive.

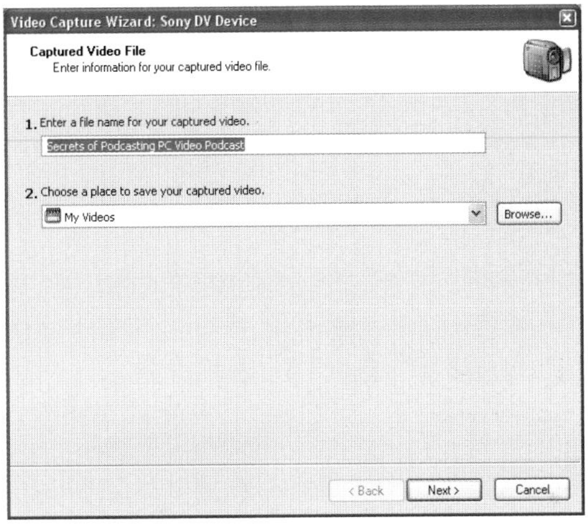

Figure 4.28

In the Video Capture Wizard, enter the name of the video, and choose where you want to save it.

When that's done, you must go through a few more steps (**Figures 4.29** through **4.32**) to get the video streaming onto your machine.

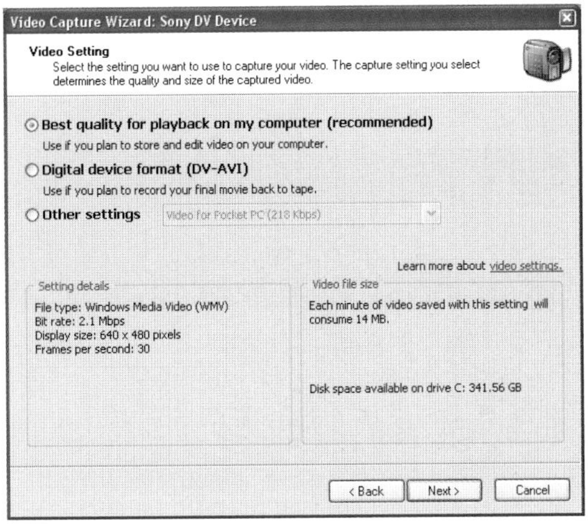

Figure 4.29

Choose the quality you desire. Unless hard drive space is an issue, choose Best Quality for Playback on My Computer, because you can change the size and/or quality of the finished product later.

Figure 4.30

Next, you get to choose whether the entire tape will be entered automatically or whether you'll choose which bits to import yourself.

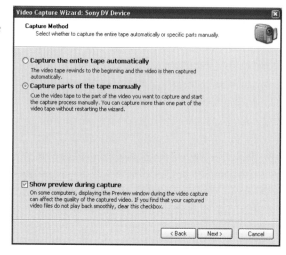

Figure 4.31

Now you get buttons that allow you to control your camcorder right from the wizard (below the heading DV Camera Controls on the right side of the window). Check the Create Clips When Wizard Finishes check box; then click the Start Capture button.

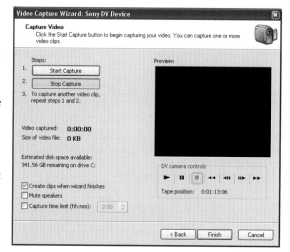

Figure 4.32

When the video you wanted to import has been imported, click the Stop Capture button and then the Finish button. When you click Finish, Movie Maker 2 imports the files, and you see this window as it does so.

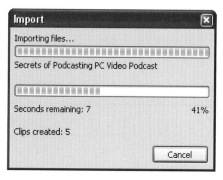

4. Import pictures or audio (if needed)

Next, you can import any audio files that you want to include. If you have a voice-over for the video that you created as a separate audio podcast, for example, you can import it now by clicking the Import Audio or Music link below Capture Video on the left side of the screen (**Figure 4.33**).

 tip You most certainly do not have to import this content at this point, however; in fact, you can go back at any point and insert audio tracks. The same goes for any pictures you want to include; you can import them at any point by clicking the Import Pictures link.

Figure 4.33

Click the Import Audio or Music link to import any sound files you want to include.

When you click the Import Audio or Music link, the Import File dialog box opens. Select the audio files you want to import (**Figure 4.34**), and click Import. These files show up as audio files in the clips area of the Movie Maker window (**Figure 4.35**) and can be dragged down to the timeline area of the window (**Figure 4.36**) at any time. When the files are in the timeline area, you can edit them and adjust the volume.

Figure 4.34

Choose which audio files to import.

Figure 4.35

The clips area.

Figure 4.36

The timeline area.

5. Place video segments in the timeline area

Now that all your video clips are sitting in the clips area, you can drag them one at a time into the timeline area at the bottom of the window. To add clips, you need only grab the clips you want to insert and drag them down to the timeline (**Figure 4.37**).

Figure 4.37
Add clips to the timeline area.

When the clips are in place, you can view them in the player window on the right side of the window (**Figure 4.38**). The timeline shows exactly how long each clip is; the storyboard at the bottom of the window shows the first frame of each clip and the transitions between clips (**Figure 4.39**).

Figure 4.38
The player window on the right side of the Movie Maker window is where you can view each clip.

Figure 4.39
The storyboard at the bottom of the window shows the first frame of each clip and the transitions between clips.

6. Add text and digital effects

If you want to gussy up the video with professional-looking transitions and digital effects, now is the time to do it. If you're going to be adding digital effects and text to particular video clips, you *must* do this before you put the transitions in place. To add a digital effect, follow the directions in **Figure 4.40** and **Figure 4.41**.

Figure 4.40

Choose Tools > Video Effects to open the Video Effects window.

Figure 4.41

There are 28 effects to choose among. To add an effect, simply drag it from the Video Effects window to the clip you want to apply it to. When the effect is applied, the result appears in the player window on the right side of the screen. In this case, I added Film Age, Old to a clip.

After you've added all the digital/visual effects that you want, it's time to add any text that you might want to use in the video. This can include credits, titles, or even music video–type headers that simply tell the audience who is being interviewed.

Figure 4.42
Click Make Titles
and Credits.

To add text, click the Make Titles and Credits link below Edit Movie on the left side of the screen (**Figure 4.42**). At this point, you get to choose when you are going to insert the title or credit: at the beginning of the movie, before a clip, on a clip, after a clip, or as credits at the end of the movie (**Figure 4.43**).

Finally, you come to the Enter Text for Title window (**Figure 4.44**). The text you enter here is shown to you as a preview in the player window on the right side of the screen (**Figure 4.45**). When you're finished, click Done, Add Title to Movie. That's it!

Figure 4.43
You get to choose where
to put the text.

Figure 4.44
Enter the text here.

Figure 4.45
When the text is
entered, it's previewed
in the player window
on the right.

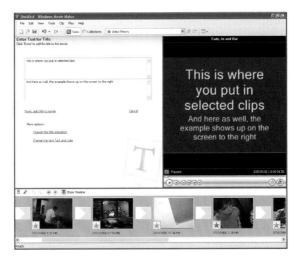

7. Insert transitions

In my opinion, video transitions are what make a presentation look really professional. A *transition* is simply how the video flows or changes from one video clip to another. There are hundreds of ways to do this, and Movie Maker 2 has 64 built-in transitions to help you spice up your production. This section (**Figure 4.46** through **Figure 4.49**) walks you through the process of inserting transitions between video clips.

Figure 4.46

Choose Tools > Video Transitions to open the Video Transitions window.

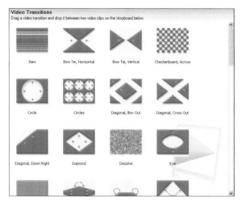

Figure 4.47

There are a whopping 64 transitions to choose among.

Figure 4.48

Drag the transition into the box between the clips in the storyboard.

Figure 4.49

The transitions can be previewed in the player window on the right. This shows a transition in action!

8. Adjust audio levels and clean up

You're nearly there. Now it's time to go into timeline mode, line up your audio portions with your video portions, and adjust the various audio levels to get your video podcast perfect. **Figure 4.50** through **Figure 4.54** show you how to adjust these levels.

Figure 4.50

Select timeline mode.

Figure 4.51 Add any extra audio you want and then drag it along the timeline to line it up appropriately. This includes background music.

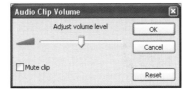

Figure 4.52 You can adjust the volume of each clip by pressing Ctrl+U to open the Audio Clip Volume dialog box.

Figure 4.53 Choose Tools > Audio Levels to open the Audio Levels window, which allows you to control the overall audio level between the video's audio track and any supplementary tracks you may have added.

Figure 4.54

You can also mute, fade in, or fade out of any audio track by right-clicking the track and choosing the appropriate command from the context menu.

> **tip**
>
> Movie Maker 2 has a Narrate Timeline function that allows you to record your audio right over the video as you watch it. For some video podcasters, this is the perfect tool. When you do this, you should use a quality microphone (see Chapter 3) and a script to ensure that you sound as professional and relaxed as possible while recording.

9. Save the movie and send it to the Web

To finish, you need to save your movie and then export it in a format that can be used for vodcasting. **Figure 4.55** through **Figure 4.58** show you how to wrap up the process.

Figure 4.55

Save the project first (choose File > Save).

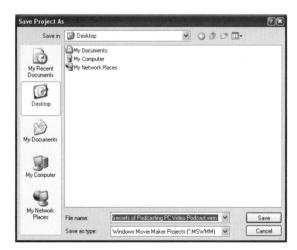

Figure 4.56

Below the Finish Movie heading in the Movie Maker window, click Send to the Web.

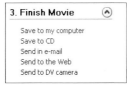

Figure 4.57

In the Save Movie Wizard, choose what size you want the movie to be.

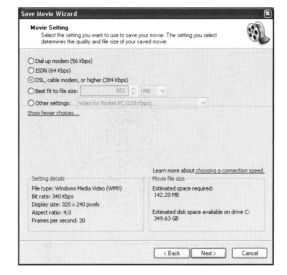

Figure 4.58

The movie will be converted, and you're done.

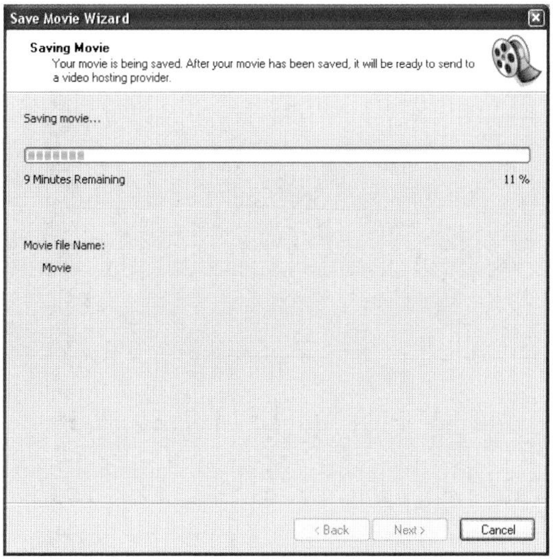

Creating a Video Podcast on a Macintosh

For this tutorial, I'm using iMovie HD 6 partly because of its ubiquitous nature in the Macintosh community, but also because it's an awesome piece of software that is both easy to use and extremely powerful. iMovie really is the standard for entry-level video editing software, and working with it is always a treat.

1. Connect the equipment

To connect a digital video camera to a computer, you need either of two connectors: a USB 2.0 connector or an IEEE 1394 FireWire connector. Both of these connectors are high-bandwidth connections, meaning that they can handle the large amount of information that must stream from the camcorder into the computer. An old-fashioned USB 1.1 connector simply isn't fast enough, so you must have either USB 2.0 or FireWire. In this case, I'm using a FireWire connection from my Sony digital Handycam (**Figure 4.59**) to my dual-processor Macintosh G5, which has a FireWire and USB 2.0 connector right on the front (**Figure 4.60**).

Figure 4.59
A Sony digital camcorder (in this case, a DCR-TRV350).

Figure 4.60
A nice shiny Macintosh with jacks on the front.

To connect the camcorder and the computer, you need the correct cable, which can be purchased separately but often comes with the camcorder. In this case, it's an IEEE 1394 cable (**Figure 4.61**). Start by connecting one end of the cable to the camcorder (**Figure 4.62**) and the other end to the computer (**Figure 4.63**).

Figure 4.61
An IEEE 1394 cable.

Figure 4.62
Connect the IEEE 1394 cable to the camcorder.

Figure 4.63
Connect the other end of the IEEE 1394 cable to the computer's FireWire jack. (Some computers have this jack on the back.)

2. Start the software and turn on the camcorder

Next, you need to open iMovie (**Figure 4.64**) and power up your camcorder into VCR mode (**Figure 4.65**). As soon as iMovie starts, it will "see" and take control of the camcorder.

Figure 4.64

Open iMovie.

Figure 4.65

Set your camcorder to VCR mode.

3. Import the video into iMovie

To import video into iMovie, you need to flick the switch in the iMovie window from edit mode to camera mode (**Figure 4.66**). After you do this, the view screen turns blue, and you have a nice little Import button at the bottom center of the screen (**Figure 4.67**).

Figure 4.66
Switch the switch to camera mode.

Figure 4.67
Click the Import button to start importing video from the camcorder to iMovie.

When the video is importing, you can start and stop it at your leisure, controlling the camcorder completely from within iMovie, or you can let the video flow into iMovie on its own. Either way, the video flows into iMovie and appears as clips in the palette on the right side of the window (**Figure 4.68**).

Figure 4.68
The clips accrue in the palette area on the right side of the iMovie window.

4. Import pictures

If you want to import pictures into your video creation, you can do so directly from iPhoto by clicking the Media button below the clips palette (**Figure 4.69**). The Media Browser opens. Click the Photos button at the top, and a selection of photos from your iPhoto library appears (**Figure 4.70**).

Figure 4.69

Click the Media button below the clips palette.

Figure 4.70

When you click the Photos button, your entire iPhoto library becomes available to you.

Click a photo, and it appears in the main window (**Figure 4.71**) along with a transparent Photo Settings dialog box (**Figure 4.72**) that allows you to apply the Ken Burns Effect to the photo. After you apply the effect (or not), you can drop the photograph into the timeline exactly where you want it (**Figure 4.73**). In this way, you can create some truly spectacular slide shows with zooming pictures that have real emotional power.

Figure 4.71

The photo you select appears in the main window.

Figure 4.72

Photo Settings is a powerful feature that allows you to use and control the Ken Burns Effect on all your photographs.

Figure 4.73

Drop the photos into the timeline to create a cool slide show.

The Ken Burns Effect

Ken Burns is a famous American documentary filmmaker, perhaps best known for his *The Civil War* documentary. Because there is no film footage from the Civil War, Burns used still photographs of the day and gave them life by slowly zooming in and out of photographs. He also panned from one image in a photograph to another, giving what would otherwise be a dull medium some much-needed motion. This style of panning and zooming in photographs has become known as the Ken Burns Effect, and Apple has included it in its iMovie software. The result is that photographic slide shows have new emotional depth and interest. The effect is really quite dramatic and has to be seen to be fully appreciated.

5. Import audio

As with importing photographs, you can import audio files by clicking the Audio button (**Figure 4.74**), which sits right beside the Photo button in the Media Browser.

Figure 4.74
Audio files are also available from the Media Browser.

When it comes to audio, you can import songs you've created in GarageBand or audio portions of a podcast that you've already created and placed in iTunes. You can also import any audio file in your iTunes library (**Figure 4.75**). When the audio file is imported, it appears in one of the two supplementary audio tracks in the timeline below the video clips (**Figure 4.76**).

Figure 4.75
The entire iTunes library is at your disposal.

Figure 4.76
There are two extra audio streams that you can place audio files in.

> **tip** You can also record a new audio track right in iMovie as you watch the video. The Microphone control and Record button appear at the bottom of the Media Browser.

6. Edit individual segments

If you want to trim individual segments or clips of video, you can do it simply by clicking the video clip (whether in the palette or the timeline) and then using the cutting tool at the bottom of the main window (**Figure 4.77**) to trim the portion of the clip you want to eliminate. You can also split clips at the playhead (**Figure 4.78**) if you want to divide a large clip into smaller components.

Figure 4.77

You can cut clips in the main window to trim them as you see fit. Use the little arrows along the bottom of the screen. The yellow line at the bottom shows what part of the clip is selected.

Figure 4.78

You can split clips whenever the playhead is located by choosing Edit > Split Video Clip at Playhead.

7. Place video segments in the timeline area

Now that everything is recorded, drag and drop the video clips into the timeline as you see fit (**Figure 4.79**). In iMovie, you can intersperse photos and video clips as much as you want, but be warned that you usually have to do this carefully to make it work well.

Figure 4.79

Drop your clips into the timeline.

When the segments are in the timeline, you can adjust the zoom (bottom-left corner) to look at just the portion of the video you want to see (**Figure 4.80**).

Figure 4.80

Zoom in or out as you see fit.

8. Add text and digital effects

If you want to gussy up the video with professional-looking transitions and digital effects, now is the time to do it. If you're going to be adding digital effects and text to particular video clips, you *must* do this before you put the transitions in place. To add a digital effect, follow the directions in **Figures 4.81, 4.82**, and **4.83**.

Figure 4.81
Click the Editing button below the clips palette.

Figure 4.82
Click the Video FX button at the top of the Editing window.

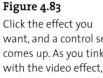

Figure 4.83
Click the effect you want, and a control set comes up. As you tinker with the video effect, a real-time preview of the effect on the selected video clip appears in the large window. If you want to keep the effect, click the Apply button in the bottom-right corner.

After you've added all the digital/visual effects that you want, it's time to add any text that you might want to use in the video. This can include credits, titles, or even music video-type headers that simply tell the audience who is being interviewed.

In the same Editing window, click the Titles button (**Figure 4.84**) to get to the Titles area. There are plenty of great options that you can fool with in the Titles area. You need to select the specific title option you want, then type in your text, then pick up the actual title icon and drag it to the timeline where you want the text/title to be inserted. So, once the text is written, select the title icon and then drag the title you want to the clip where you want to insert it or to the place you want to insert it, if you're dealing with credits on a black background (**Figure 4.85**).

Figure 4.84
Click the Titles button.

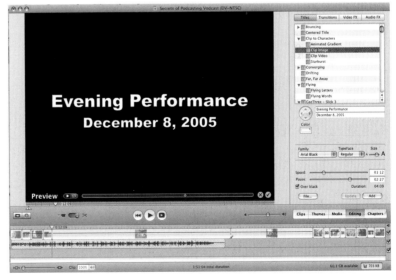

Figure 4.85 As you type the text you want to use, it's previewed in the main window dynamically. To insert the title, drag the title name (in this case, Clip Image) into the place on the timeline where you want it to go; the title will be inserted there.

9. Insert transitions

In my opinion, video transitions are what make the presentation look really professional. A *transition* is simply how the video flows or changes from one video clip to another. There are hundreds of ways to do this, and iMovie offers many ways to do this. My version of iMovie has the complete Slick series of transitions from GeeThree, so I have the ability to do some pretty special transitions. This section (**Figure 4.86** through **Figure 4.89**) walks you through the process of inserting transitions between video clips.

Figure 4.86

Click the Transitions button at the top of the Editing window.

Figure 4.87

Set the playhead between the clips you want to transition between; then select the transition you want to see by clicking it in the Transitions window.

Figure 4.88

Preview the transition. The preview happens automatically when you click the transition icon (in the Transitions window) that you are interested in. It's a cool feature; you simply click the transition you want, and the preview occurs automatically. In this way, you can preview many transitions quickly.

Figure 4.89

Drag the transition down to the place where you want it to go, and the computer will work on inserting it.

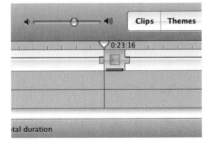

10. Adjust audio levels

When all the video clips are in place, and the transitions and titles are in place, you need only drop in any needed audio and adjust the audio levels. You can adjust the audio levels simply by clicking the stream (be it video or audio) in the timeline (**Figure 4.90**), grabbing the line that runs through the clip, and then dragging the line to whatever level you desire (**Figure 4.91**).

Figure 4.90

Click the feed on which you want to adjust the volume.

Figure 4.91 Drag the little line up or down to adjust the volume. You can adjust the volume in minute and gradual ways by using this system.

Note that the line that runs through each clip can be grabbed anywhere, and each time you click the line, a new point (a dot) appears on the line. In this way, you can make points between which audio can be skewed up or down gradually or sharply. You can have as much or as little control of the audio of a stream as you want. If you want the audio of a stream to be set globally, grab the line right at the beginning of the clip (on the far left) and pull it down; the result is that the audio level for that entire clip goes down with it.

When all the levels are just how you want them, the video podcast is complete (**Figure 4.92**).

Figure 4.92

If you want to get into the nitty-gritty of a particular clip, you can click the Audio FX button in the Editing window. In the Audio FX pane, you can add audio effects such as reverb, delay, and pitch changes, and even use a graphic equalizer to refine the sound of a particular clip.

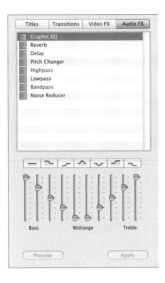

11. Save the movie and export it

To finish, you need to save your movie and then export it in a format that can be used for vodcasting. **Figure 4.93** through **Figure 4.99** show you how to wrap up the process.

Figure 4.93

Save the project first (choose File > Save Project).

Figure 4.94

Choose File > Export.

Figure 4.95

In the next window, choose Expert Settings from the Compress Movie For drop-down menu; then click the Share button.

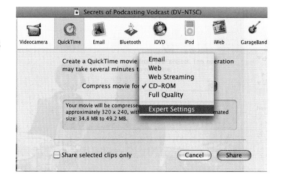

Figure 4.96

From the Export drop-down menu in the next window, choose the level of export you want; then start the process by clicking the Save button.

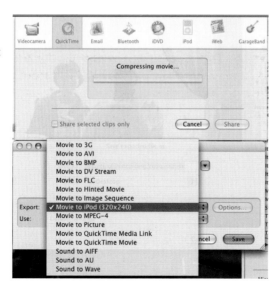

Figure 4.97

If you want to send the video podcast directly to iWeb, click the iWeb icon.

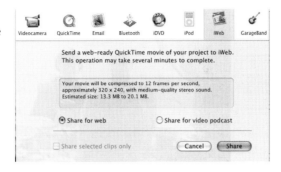

Figure 4.98

If you're sending to iWeb, select Share for Video Podcast and click the Share button.

Figure 4.99

At this point, the video is compressed; then it's moved to iWeb automatically!

For a tutorial on publishing a video podcast, check out Chapter 5. There, you can find everything you need to know about publishing your podcasts, be they audio or video.

5

Podcast Distribution

OK, so you have put together a podcast that's going to set the world on fire. You spent hours coming up with witty and erudite discourse between the host and co-host. Important and compelling guests were interviewed at just the right time during the podcast, and everything went swimmingly. Heck, even Peter Gabriel decided that he would allow you to use some of his music in the background. The editing process is complete, and the shiny new podcast is all ready to be heard (or watched) by the masses!

There's only one catch: Knowledge of how to publish your podcast on the World Wide Web eludes you. Not to worry, because this chapter details the intricacies of using the RSS specification so that your podcast can reach the maximum number of people with the least amount of effort. Although *RSS* actually stands for *Really Simple Syndication,* for a nonscripting or programming newbie, the term "really simple" doesn't exactly jump to mind when learning RSS from scratch. Fortunately, several programs have emerged that make the process of publishing podcasts with RSS a relatively simple one. Indeed, in the months since the first edition of *Secrets of Podcasting* was released, several new alternatives for Web publication have come to light, making the process even easier. One easy-to-use new program is Apple's iWeb, which—in conjunction with GarageBand, iTunes, iMovie, and even iPhoto—allows you to create and publish a podcast with very little fuss.

This chapter covers podcasting distribution options, from the complex options that appeal to the programmer personality to the all-in-one packages that completely demystify the process. The routes this chapter examines are

- RSS file construction: building an RSS feed from scratch

- Alternative podcast distribution: MP3 files and streaming audio

- Web-site packagers: companies that charge a fee to do it all for you

- Software packages: software, like FeedForAll, that makes publishing an RSS feed an automated process

The chapter also looks at how to get your podcast out there and noticed (**Figure 5.1**). No matter what route you choose to take with regard to creating RSS feeds, this chapter has all the information you need to make the process second nature.

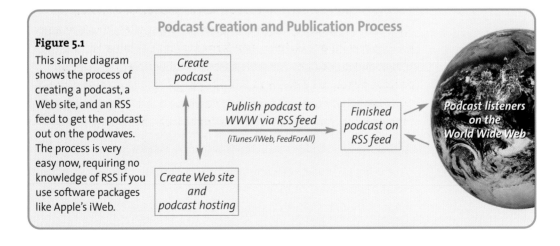

Podcast Creation and Publication Process

Figure 5.1

This simple diagram shows the process of creating a podcast, a Web site, and an RSS feed to get the podcast out on the podwaves. The process is very easy now, requiring no knowledge of RSS if you use software packages like Apple's iWeb.

Create podcast

Publish podcast to WWW via RSS feed
(iTunes/iWeb, FeedForAll)

Finished podcast on RSS feed

Podcast listeners on the World Wide Web

Create Web site and podcast hosting

RSS

RSS, or *Really Simple Syndication,* is the engine behind the podcasting phenomenon. The RSS standard is what enabled the relatively simple proliferation and dissemination of podcasts throughout the world. RSS is defined as a standard set of tools for the purpose of allowing frequent updates for content on the World Wide Web. In short, RSS is a XML-based format for content distribution over the World Wide Web. Using RSS, a Webmaster (or podcaster) can place content on a blog or podcast Web site in such a way that news or podcatchers (programs that search for new content) can grab the fresh content in a concise manner.

note

What the heck is XML? *XML* stands for *Extensible Markup Language.* First, though, you need to know what a markup language is. A *markup language* combines text and extra information about the text in a file that can be used to perform a function. A good example of a markup language is HTML (Hypertext Markup Language), which is the backbone of every page on the World Wide Web. Extensible Markup Language (XML) is designed to help mediate the sharing of data across different kinds of systems, such as those present on the Internet. In summary, XML is a type of language that allows information to flow freely through different systems across the Internet without difficulty.

RSS means that consumers can use programs like iPodder or HappyFish and have them scour hundreds of podcast Web sites in minutes, downloading *only* what is new on those sites. In this manner, RSS has revolutionized the way information is disseminated, and that includes podcasts. For podcasters, RSS allows them to place a podcast out on the Web for millions of people to access. For consumers, RSS allows them to have access to a nearly unlimited amount of content while saving them from having to look for the content one item at a time.

A Brief History of RSS

Really Simple Syndication was originally designed by Netscape back in 1999. Eventually, Dave Winder added features to RSS, including the Scripting News SML format. In 2002, RSS 2.0 was proposed, and that is the standard used today. RSS 2.0 is published under a Creative Commons license at the Berkman Center for Internet & Society at Harvard University.

From an actual line-by-line explanation of an RSS Enclosure to a tutorial on how to create your own, this section delves into the nitty-gritty of the Really Simple Syndication standard and how it works. I need to point out that there are entire books (many of them, in fact) that cover just RSS and how it works. That said, I will attempt to give you enough information to feel comfortable with the format and to use it on a basic level for podcast publishing. If you want to learn more about RSS online, check out the Berkman Center site at http://blogs.law.harvard.edu/tech/rss.

In the following sections, I first go through the process of creating an RSS file for a podcasting feed. Then I list the completed file with an explanation of each and every line in the file. By following through these two sections, you will have a decent understanding of how RSS works. The example I set out can even be a template for your own RSS file.

Creating an RSS feed

Anyone who has some experience coding in HTML will likely find RSS relatively easy to understand. By comparison, anyone who has never done any HTML coding will likely find RSS a little cryptic despite what the acronym implies.

 In this tutorial, I refer to RSS files with regard to podcasts and podcasts alone. RSS feeds can be created for many kinds of information, but for the sake of simplicity and the spirit of this podcasting book, everything I discuss refers to podcasts.

Needed: Web Site

To create an RSS file or feed, you need a Web page with space to store the podcast. That page will need to be able to handle the bandwidth if the podcast becomes successful and thousands of people download it. If you are serious about podcasting, setting up a Web site for your show is a necessity, both as a contact point for your fan base and also as a syndication point for getting your podcasts out on the World Wide Web.

Obtaining a Web site is remarkably easy, and many ISP services supply easy-to-construct online tools for creating a Web page without any knowledge of HTML. Conversely, if you are knowledgeable in the ways of HTML, you might want to create a Web site from scratch. Many design tools—such as GoLive (Adobe), FrontPage (Microsoft), and Dreamweaver (Macromedia)—are decent choices for creating a Web site.

If money is no object, plenty of Web-design houses all over the world are champing at the bit to design Web sites of all kinds. Finally, the boom in podcasting has led to the emergence of several podcast-hosting Web sites that enable you to publish your podcast for a fee (see "Web-Site Packagers" later in this chapter).

 When your podcast is all set up and the RSS feed is in place, I suggest that you put the RSS and XML icons on your Web site. These two tiny icons tell the world that you have a syndicated podcast feed that can be accessed by a podcatcher program (aggregator).

Found: iWeb

iWeb is part of Apple's iLife '06 software suite, which includes iTunes, iPhoto, iMovie, iDVD, and GarageBand. This group of programs is an all-in-one package that supplies everything you need to produce and publish quality audio or video podcasts. iWeb makes publishing a podcast ridiculously simple, even to the extent that it makes the creation of the RSS feed 100 percent invisible to the user. A few clicks of the mouse are all that's needed to publish a podcast in the iTunes directory. Check out "Publishing a Podcast with iWeb" later in this chapter.

The catch? This software suite is available only for the Mac, so those of you using Windows PCs (the vast majority of computer users on the planet) are out of luck when it comes to iLife '06. Not to worry, however, because there are several easy-to-use products for the Windows crowd as well.

To begin, I'll explain what an RSS file is: quite simply, a set of *tags* (instructions) that name, explain, and point to a podcast. In addition, these tags set up parameters for other details, such as how often people can check the feeds and whether to allow a failed download of the podcast to restart. There are other elements of an RSS file, of course, but not to worry; I'll go through them in detail one at a time.

Conventions

The RSS language has certain conventions that you need to be aware of:

- All tags are *closed*—enclosed between the characters < and >. The tag `<title>`, for example, means that all text following this tag will be represented as the title of the podcast.

- Every instruction that you enter must also be closed. In `<title>Bart's Podcast</title>`, for example, `<title>` means "Start the title here," with the words *Bart's Podcast* being the title; then the `</title>` tag instructs the program to close the title (**Figure 5.2**). The forward slash before the tag signifies that this is the end of the instruction. Every instruction must be closed after it is opened. In the sample file, which you'll create in the following section, `<channel>` at the beginning of the file is closed with a `</channel>` tag at the end of the file.

Figure 5.2

This is a breakdown of each element in one line of an RSS file.

This is the actual title of the podcast that the end user will see.

`<title>Bart's Podcast</title>`

Instruction to begin the title text

Instruction to end the title

RSS files can constructed with high-end features that can be fairly complicated when the full range of instructions (tags) and features is implemented. It is not in the scope of this book to explore RSS and XML in depth, so I have kept the process as simple as possible. Therefore, for the purposes of creating a simple RSS feed, the following instructions are all that you need:

`<rss version="2.0">` identifies the files as RSS 2.0 files.

`<channel>` is an instruction that sets up an area where information about the feed goes. This information includes the show's title, the Web page's URL, copyright information, and several other factors.

`<title>` identifies the title text for the show.

`<link>` identifies the link to the podcast's Web site.

`<description>` identifies the descriptive text for the show.

`<lastBuildDate>` identifies the last time the file was altered.

`<language>` identifies what language the programming is in (English, Spanish, German, and so on).

`<copyright>` establishes the copyright of the podcast content.

`<generator>` identifies who created the file.

`<webmaster>` identifies the Webmaster for the podcast's Web site.

`<ttl>` means *time to live*. This value instructs the RSS readers (such as iPodder and HappyFish) how often they can look to see whether new content is available on this feed.

`<item>` is a podcast feed. It can also be a feed to a text file, video file, or anything else. For purposes of this book, however, it refers to a podcast feed.

`<enclosure>` links to the actual MP3 file and also establishes the file's length and type.

The instructions such as `<channel>` **are commonly referred to as** *tags*. **The proper way to describe them is to call them** *elements*, **but because the term** *tags* **is ubiquitous, that's what I use here.**

Creating the file

This section takes you through the process of creating an RSS file for the purposes of publishing a single podcast. I assume that you have already set up a Web site and that the podcast is already linked on the site.

The first section of the RSS file contains information such as the show's title, the copyright information, the Web site for the show, and the *ttl (time to live)* value. Following is a step-by-step walkthrough of each line of the RSS file.

 The file names and links used in this sample are not real links. They are for demonstration purposes only.

1. First, the RSS file needs to be identified. The first line of the code identifies the files as an RSS file.

   ```
   <rss version="2.0">
   ```

2. The next entry is `<channel>`, which acts as a marker that begins the information about the podcasting feed.

   ```
   <channel>
   ```

3. The next two lines show the feed (or show) title and the URL of the show's Web site, respectively.

   ```
   <title>Secrets of Podcasting</title>
   <link>
    http://www.peechpitpress.com/secretsofpodcasting/
   </link>
   ```

4. Next up is the description text for the show. Note again that the description instruction is started and then closed after the descriptive text.

   ```
   <description>
    The best podcast about a podcast book in the world!
   </description>
   ```

5. The next two lines show the last time the RSS file was edited and establish the language in which the RSS file is written (English, Spanish, and so on).

```
<lastBuildDate>Mon, 9 May 2006 22:19:41 -0400
 </lastBuildDate>
<language>en-us</language>
```

6. The next two lines show copyright information and the identity of the creator of the file.

```
<copyright>Copyright 2006</copyright>
<generator>Bart</generator>
```

7. The next line contains the contact information for the Webmaster of the Web site where the podcast file resides or is hosted.

```
<webMaster>JerryG@bogusaddress.com</webMaster>
```

8. The final line before the nitty-gritty of the actual podcast feed involves something called time to live (ttl). Time to live is important because it tells aggregators (podcast readers) how often they are allowed to check to see whether a new feed is available. I suggest that you set the ttl to at least 60 minutes; otherwise, your server could get hammered by people checking every minute. Setting the ttl to 60 minutes ultimately saves bandwidth as well, which usually translates into cash in your pocket.

```
<ttl>60</ttl>
```

The next portion of the RSS file deals with the actual podcast feed information, which is classified as an <item>. If you were placing several podcasts in the feed, each podcast would have its own <item> section like this one.

9. The first line is an <item> line, which signifies a distinct podcast. If there are multiple podcasts in a feed, each one will have a section beginning with <item> and ending with </item>.

```
<item>
```

10. The next line is the title of the podcast. In the case of a weekly or daily podcast, this line would contain the name of the episode.

```
<title>Secrets of Podcasts Show #1</title>
```

11. Now you need to show the link to the actual MP3 file (or other type of audio file). A link is signified with the `<link>` tag.

```
<link>http://www.peechpitpress.com/secretsofPC.mp3
 </link>
```

12. The next line describes the podcast (or episode).

```
<description>Learn how to podcast!</description>
```

13. Next up are the publication date and time. The date is self explanatory, and it is worth noting that the time is on a 24-hour clock (22:41 = 10:41 p.m.). The `-0600` at the end denotes the time zone—in this case, minus 6 hours from GMT (Greenwich Mean Time). The most important thing to remember with the time zone is to be consistent from feed to feed with whatever time zone you select.

```
<pubDate>Sat, 13 May 2006 22:41:10 -0600</pubDate>
```

14. The next portion is perhaps the most important. This part is called the *enclosure,* and it is the link that the podcatching software will download. The most important aspect of the enclosure statement is to ensure that the length of the audio file (in this case, an MP3 file) is exactly correct. The length is represented in bytes, and if this value is correct, it allows podcatching software to resume an interrupted download, which can help reduce bandwidth in the long run. Last, the `type` parameter is important because it describes exactly what kind of audio file you are using and, therefore, ensures the proper handling of the MP3 file after it is downloaded by a listener.

```
<enclosure url= "
 http://www.peechpitpress.com/secretsofPC.mp3"
length="38998016" type="audio/mpeg"/>
```

15. That's it. Now that the item is complete, you just need to close out the item, the channel, and the RSS file as follows.

```
</item>
</channel>
</rss>
```

The finished file

Following is the complete file, all ready to go. At a glance, the RSS file in this form can be a daunting thing for someone with no experience in HTML coding. After you go through it line by line, however, reading an explanation for each line, it really isn't that bad. In fact, you could use this file as a template for any RSS file meant for publishing a podcast.

```
<rss version="2.0">
<channel>
  <title>Secrets of Podcasting</title>
  <link>
    http://www.peechpitpress.com/secretsofpodcasting/
  </link>
<description>
  The best podcast about a podcast book in the world!
</description>
<lastBuildDate>Mon, 9 May 2006 22:19:41 -0400
  </lastBuildDate>
<language>en-us</language>
  <copyright>Copyright 2006</copyright>
  <generator>Bart</generator>
  <webMaster>JerryG@bogusaddress.com</webMaster>
  <ttl>60</ttl>
<item>
  <title>Secrets of Podcasts Show #1</title>
  <link>http://www.peechpitpress.com/secretsofPC.mp3
  </link>
  <description>Learn how to podcast!</description>
  <pubDate>Sat, 13 May 2006 22:41:10 -600</pubDate>
  <enclosure url=
    " http://www.peechpitpress.com/secretsofPC.mp3"
  length="38998016" type="audio/mpeg"/>
</item>
</channel>
</rss>
```

Figure 5.3 shows the basic flow of how a podcast is created and distributed to the world. Sometimes, it's nice to have colorful, easy-to-read representations like this.

Figure 5.3

The process of creating and publishing a podcast.

Create your
podcast

Get a Web
page to host
your podcast

Create the
RSS feed

Now the world
can enjoy your
podcast!

Putting the RSS file to use

Now that the RSS file is complete, you have a couple more tasks left to get things up and running. The up side is that the hard part is over; this portion of the process is not particularly difficult, but it needs to be reviewed nonetheless. The following steps take the process through to completion:

1. Name your file—for this example, Secrets.xml.

The .xml extension isn't actually necessary, but it's standard, so just go with the flow.

2. Next, place the file on your Web site (or wherever your podcasting feed is being hosted).

This will end up looking something like http://www.bogus address.com/Secrets.xml.

3. As a test, try to open that file directly from your browser.

Most likely, a warning will flash across your screen, complaining that the file is not a valid HTML file, but that isn't a problem. What should happen is that the file you worked on appears in the window (**Figure 5.4**). This means that the link works!

Figure 5.4

When you use a Web browser to go to the RSS feed link, it should look something like this.

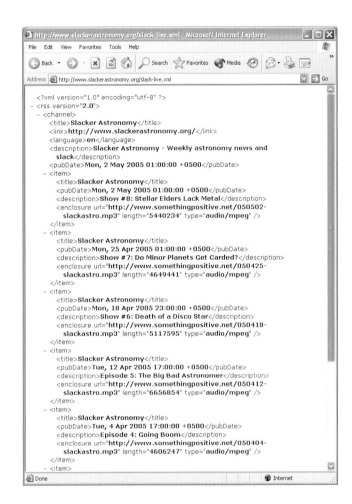

4. Launch a podcast aggregator (a podcatcher program) such as iTunes, iPodder, or HappyFish, and paste your link into the New Feed box.

   If the software goes to the site and downloads your podcast, you've done it!

Telling the world about your podcast

Next up, you must tell the world that your podcast exists. There are quite a few ways to get the word out—so many, in fact, that it's difficult to list them all. That said, there are a few tried-and-true methods for getting your podcast on the radar of the podcasting community, including using blog advertising channels and using Web sites to aid in your cause.

Weblogs.com

One of the first places to go is a Web site called Weblogs.com (http://audio.weblogs.com). This site is one of the best places to get your podcast listed. The site has a specific page that allows you to enter the podcast feed link and the URL of your Web page. After you do this, your podcast will appear on Weblogs.com. There is also a handy Feed Validation feature (**Figure 5.5**) that allows you to check your RSS code right on the spot.

Figure 5.5

The Weblogs.com "feed validation" page is an easy way to test your RSS code.

Contact the community

Contact the main podcasting Web sites, including www.podcast alley.com, www.podcastingnews.com, and www.podcastbunker.com (**Figure 5.6**). Each of these sites has an "add your podcast" link that allows you to get your podcast feed out there so that listeners can find it and give your show a listen. Check out the appendix of this book for a list of podcasting Web sites that you can contact to help distribute your podcast.

Figure 5.6

Scores of Web sites can help you get the word out on your podcast.

iTunes Podcast Directory

A button smack dab in the middle of the iTunes Music Store's Podcasts page says Submit a Podcast. When you click this button, you are taken to a page (**Figure 5.7**) where you need only enter the RSS feed URL to be added to the iTunes Podcast Directory, along with tens of thousands of other podcasts. After the podcast is submitted, it's checked for appropriateness before being officially added to the directory. When it's in the directory, however, it's there to stay, and millions of people instantly have access to your podcast! The iTunes Podcast Directory is arguably one of the best places to get attention for your podcast.

Figure 5.7

The iTunes Podcast Directory is *the* place to list your podcast. It's also dead easy to submit a podcast to be listed.

Podcast Alley Podcast Directory

Like the iTunes Podcast Directory, the Podcast Alley Podcast Directory (**Figure 5.8**) is an excellent place to have your podcast listed. Podcast Alley was the first cohesive Web site about podcasting that brought everything together effectively in one place. When this chapter was written, Podcast Alley's podcast database listed about 1,000 more podcasts than the iTunes directory, but when you're talking about tens of thousands of podcasts, it's really a moot point; they are both great resources.

Figure 5.8

Podcast Alley (www. podcastalley.com) also has an easy-to-use Podcast Directory tool.

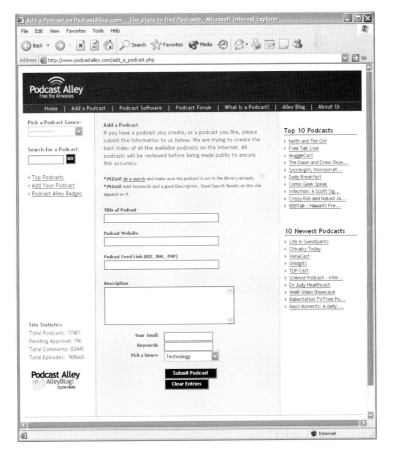

Advertise on your own Web site or on a blog

If you have your own Web site, it is a good idea to put up a banner or a note about your podcast and the feed link. If you have friends or colleagues with Web sites, you can trade with them so that they link to your podcast as well. This technique may net you some new listeners, and if they like the show, their word-of-mouth advertising will be worth the effort.

Interview with Aaron, Pamela, and Travis

"Slacker Astronomy" is a popular podcast run by Aaron, Pamela, and Travis—no last names here (**Figure 5.9**).

Aaron has a MS in astronomy and currently is in a Ph.D. program at James Cook University. He has worked for the American Association of Variable Star Observers (AAVSO) for seven years.

Pamela has a Ph.D. in astronomy. She works for Harvard University's Science Center and writes for *Sky & Telescope* magazine.

Figure 5.9
The "Slacker Astronomy" crew: Aaron, Pamela, and Travis.

Travis has a BA in broadcast journalism from Emerson College and is involved in several musical projects in addition to working at the AAVSO.

Farkas: When did you first become aware of podcasting?

SA: Aaron read about it in a newspaper article at the airport while traveling for the holidays. The article talked about mainly the religious podcasts. He thought it would be perfect for astronomy and then invited Travis and Pamela to join him, and it was the first they heard about it.

Farkas: What made you decide to create your own podcast? Was the desire to get the message out with regard to astronomy the driving force?

SA: Our Prime Directive is to have fun. We do this for ourselves first of all. A strong second is the desire to share news of astronomy while respecting the intelligence of our audience (i.e., not "dumbing" it down). Aaron and Pamela are both very active in astronomical

Interview with Aaron, Pamela, and Travis *(continued)*

education and public outreach. so this was a natural extension for them. Travis is interested in the broadcasting aspect of it as well as astronomy.

Farkas: What has surprised you the most with regard to the impact of your podcast(s)?

SA: Two things. The first is that so many people listen! We were hoping for about 500 listeners, and so far, we have ten times that. Secondly, the e-mails we get surprised us—in particular, the numbers and thoughtfulness of them. People have been very kind and supportive, and that keeps us going.

Farkas: What are your plans for "Slacker Astronomy" going forward?

SA: We have lots of ideas. We want to expand our interviews and soundseeing tours. We also have ideas to move it beyond podcasting and into public talks and other media. Finally, we want to work with more professionals and produce podcasts on demand. For example, when a professional observatory has a press release, they can contact us to produce a podcast version of it for release at the same time.

Farkas: Where do you see podcasting going in the next year? The next 5 years?

SA: The most interesting thing will be to see how the attempts at commercialism play out. We think it has equal chances to succeed or fail.

Farkas: Do you have an opinion on the commercialization of podcasting?

SA: It will depend on whether marketing agents have respect for the audience. If they don't, and they treat [the audience] as one mass, it will fail. They need to tailor their technique for each unique podcast. Our advice to marketers: Pay no attention to what others are doing, and come up with your own plan.

As for our podcast, we do not plan to become a for-profit enterprise simply because it would violate our Prime Directive: to have fun. Freedom is important to us. As soon as we have to self-censor and kiss a brass ring, the show will no longer be fun, and we doubt we could ever make enough to justify that. We did an April Fool's show where we pretended to be shut down by The Man. Our audience loved it.

Alternative Podcasting Distribution Options

RSS is the de facto dominant way to distribute podcasts over the Internet, and for most home-baked podcast creators, this is the way they go about distribution. Some commercial enterprises, however, use a couple of other methods to distribute podcasts, and those methods are what this section examines.

MP3 (or similar) files

Ultimately, when a podcast is created, it becomes an MP3, MP4, Ogg Vorbis, WAV, or AAC file. In the case of mainstream podcasting, these files are then published via RSS. Some podcasts, however, are not set up with RSS but are instead available as straight downloads in the form of MP3 files (or one of the other compression formats). Although RSS offers the most exposure for a podcast, having a simple downloadable file also has its advantages and uses.

The most common examples of downloadable MP3 files in the commercial realm are audiobooks and periodicals through sites like Audible.com (**Figure 5.10**). These sites sell content and then make the

Figure 5.10
Audible.com allows downloading of all the podcasts it sells.

content available as downloadable compressed files that can be played on many MP3 players. In the case of Audible.com, the files are also available as streaming content, but a large number of the site's customers use the download feature so that they have a copy of the podcast on their hard drives.

Corporations are increasingly making podcasts available to both the curious public and their employees. In the case of Duke University (**Figure 5.11**), educational lectures are made available as MP3 files for download by the student body. Basically, any audio file that is available as a download from a hyperlink on any Web site is considered to be a podcast.

Figure 5.11

From this portal, Duke University is using audio files to disseminate lectures to its students.

If you are creating a podcast for a company that wants only a select group of people to hear it, placing the podcast in a hyperlink for individual download may be the best route to take. Many companies and organizations include a combination of a hyperlink to the podcast file and an RSS feed and/or a streaming feed. Indeed, some podcasters have begun to make their podcasts available through multiple routes. On the site of the top-ten podcast "MuggleCast," for example, links are included for download of the podcasts, streaming podcasts, and RSS feeds (**Figure 5.12**).

Figure 5.12

"MuggleCast" is an example of a podcast that offers multiple access points.

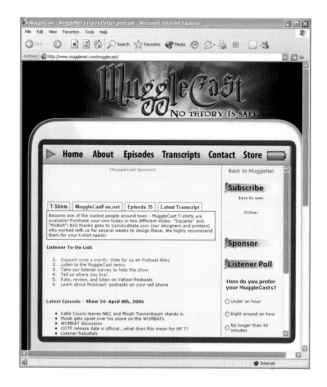

Ultimately, the most compelling reasons to link a podcast file to a hyperlink on a Web site are

- For corporations to disseminate information to their employees

- As an adjunct to publishing podcasts through RSS

- For educational institutions to make podcasts available to their students but not to the rest of the world

- For anyone who wants to control who gains access to the podcast

- For private podcasters who want only people who visit their Web sites to have access to the podcast

Streaming

Until the phenomenon of podcasting reared its head, much of the audio content on the Internet came in the form of streaming audio. *Streaming audio* is an audio feed that is downloaded dynamically (as you listen to it) from a source somewhere on the Internet to a media player on your computer. Internet radio uses this technology, as do many movie preview sites that show movie trailers. Streaming is also used by commercial Web sites like Amazon.com (where users can hear samples of songs being sold) and Audible.com (where users can listen to entire books).

Ultimately, streaming audio is not the most important pathway for getting your podcasts heard; RSS feeds are by far the best method. That said, if you want to use it, you can provide streaming audio in several ways, including:

- Formatting the file link so that it starts playing the file as soon as the link is clicked.

- Using a flash-based player on your Web site to stream the audio files.

- Using a Web service like Live365 (www.live365.com), which offers packages for hosting your material and streaming it out for you (**Figure 5.13**). The costs of sites like this vary, depending on the package and features chosen.

Figure 5.13

Sites like Live365 can stream your material if you are gung-ho on having streaming audio of your podcasts.

Nicecast

Available only for the Mac, Nicecast (www.rogueamoeba.com/nicecast; **Figure 5.14**) is an Internet broadcaster that allows users to broadcast MP3 files to the Internet via iTunes. Although it's not practical for large-scale podcasting, Nicecast is a very ingenious way to enable streaming audio from a Macintosh computer running OS X (required).

Figure 5.14

Nicecast allows Mac users to stream podcasts onto the Internet in a limited way.

The feature list of Nicecast includes

- The ability to broadcast a live event

- Via iTunes, the ability to broadcast podcasts one after another

- The ability to add voice-overs and digital effects to outgoing streaming content

Nicecast is best used by those who want to enable a few select people to stream their podcasts; this is not the answer for large-scale dissemination of a podcast. Still, at only $40, it is a very handy piece of software to have around, and it allows you to broadcast your podcasts over the Internet, if only in a limited way.

RSS Feed Software Options

If actually writing an RSS feed file is something that does not hold much appeal for you, worry not; several software options allow you to create RSS feeds with relative ease. These programs don't create the Web sites or host the space where the podcasts will reside, but they do make the process of creating the RSS file very painless.

BlogMatrix

BlogMatrix (**Figure 5.15**), the creator of Sparks! 2.0 (mentioned in Chapter 3), offers a free service for sharing your podcasts via its Web site (www.blogmatrix.com). Remember that Sparks! 2.0 is a podcast aggregator as well as an audio recorder, editor, and podcast publisher. Most of its features are free, but if you want to use the recording feature, there is a $10 fee. (The recording feature comes with a 30-day free trial.)

Figure 5.15

BlogMatrix is a solid solution for hosting podcasts.

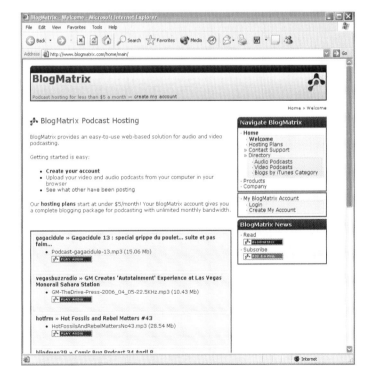

For all-in-one solutions, it's hard to beat this piece of software, but there are limitations in terms of the free BlogMatrix account and RSS feed publishing. The feed is available to other BlogMatrix users but not to the world at large. Still, this is a viable option for some podcasters.

ePodcast Producer

ePodcast Producer is a commercial product that runs $249.95 from Industrial Audio Software's Web site (www.industrialaudiosoftware.com/ products/epodcastproducer.html; **Figure 5.16**). ePodcast Producer is an all-in-one solution that is acceptable, but again, if elegance and ease of use are your goal, it may be better to put the pieces together piecemeal rather than have this all-in-one package. The one thing that ePodcast Producer does offer is the ability to create the RSS feed for your podcast with relative ease. For those who are looking for all-in-one solutions, this is on par with Propaganda.

Figure 5.16

ePodcast Producer is a commercial option that carries a commercial price.

Feeder

Published by Reinvented Software (www.reinventedsoftware.com; **Figure 5.17**), Feeder is a Macintosh RSS feed creator that makes creating an RSS feed as easy as pie. Feeder is an excellent tool for podcasters who are producing multiple podcasts on a regular basis.

Figure 5.17

Feeder is exclusive to the Mac.

The features of Feeder include

- Templates to edit and create feeds

- Preflight check that checks the feed before it's published

- Quick-start feature for creating, importing, or downloading a feed

- Ability to publish finished feeds to your server via FTP

Feeder uses a very intuitive interface to guide you through the process of creating an RSS feed. After the feed has been created, clicking the New Item button allows you to add subsequent podcast feeds with ease. For Mac users who want a simple way to create RSS feeds for their podcasts, Feeder is the No. 1 option, and at $29.95, it won't break the bank. Feeder has a 14-day free trial built in, enabling you to sample before you buy.

FeedForAll

FeedForAll (www.feedforall.com; **Figure 5.18**) is the RSS feed creator of choice right now for the PC, and with the recent release of a Macintosh version, it may give iWeb a run for its money. With a very simple wizard that asks a few questions about the podcast, the link to the podcast, and the addition of some descriptive text, FeedForAll automatically creates an RSS file that you can set up on your Web site immediately for your podcast to be published. FeedForAll is a powerful tool that allows users to create, edit, and publish RSS feeds with ease. For those with a deeper knowledge of RSS, FeedForAll allows tweaking of details that novices are likely to avoid.

Figure 5.18

FeedForAll is a great one-stop RSS feed creator.

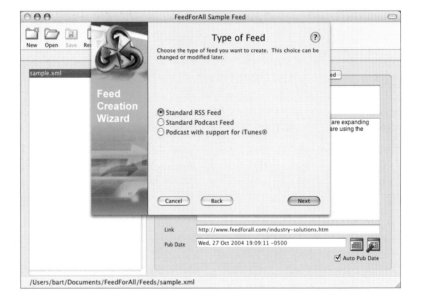

At $39.95, FeedForAll is reasonably priced for anyone who doesn't want to learn how to create RSS feeds from scratch. The features of FeedForAll include

- Spell checking

- XML editor

- Simple Feed Creation Wizard that walks users through the process step by step

- Image editor for creating RSS feed images

- Automatic feed repair option

- Automatic date management

- Support for an unlimited number of feeds

- Mac version interfaces with Apple's iTunes

- Customizable

The most appealing feature of FeedForAll is the Feed Creation Wizard. Using the wizard, you can create an RSS feed simply by answering a few questions, one of which is shown in **Figure 5.19**. For anyone who's serious about podcasting but not serious about spending time learning XML and RSS, FeedForAll is an excellent answer.

Figure 5.19

FeedForAll's Feed Creation Wizard is a snap to use.

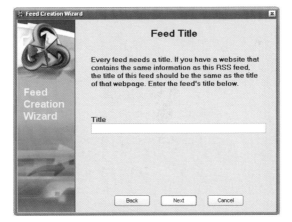

Propaganda

Mentioned in Chapter 3, Propaganda (www.makepropaganda.com; **Figure 5.20**) is an all-in-one podcast creation/publishing program that takes you from recording the podcast through editing and finally to creating and publishing the RSS feed. If an all-in-one solution is what you need, Propaganda does the job adequately. That said, there are more elegant individual pieces of software that do what Propaganda does, but the process is not confined to one piece of software.

Figure 5.20

Propaganda is a one-stop solution for podcast creation and publication.

Publishing a Podcast with iWeb

As mentioned earlier in this chapter, iWeb (**Figure 5.21**) is part of Apple's iLife '06 software suite. One of iWeb's chief capabilities is to allow the quick and truly painless publication of a podcast to the iTunes Podcast Directory via a .Mac account. Now, you don't actually have to have a .Mac account to use iWeb, but for the purposes of this tutorial, I'll assume that you do (because a free trial account is available).

Figure 5.21

iWeb is a powerful tool for publishing Web sites—and podcasts too!

OK, so you've created a podcast—an audio podcast or a video podcast; it doesn't really matter. The important thing is that you've got the podcast in your hot little hand. You've spend hours recording and refining it, and now you need to get it out to the world. I'll show you in a few easy steps how to publish your podcast by putting it on a Web page, placing the page on the Internet, and then listing your podcast in the iTunes Podcast Directory. Fortunately, it's a snap with iWeb!

.Mac

.Mac (**Figure 5.22**) is a complete Internet service that offers e-mail, 1 GB of hard disk space that can be used with iDisk (basically, an external hard drive), or Backup 3 (a way to protect your important files). The key features of .Mac for podcasters are the Photocasting services and the ability to publish podcasts via iWeb. Publishing a podcasting Web page with iWeb is so simple that it is quite literally one click; that's it. Although .Mac is aimed mainly at Macintosh enthusiasts, it does have a limited set of features for non-Mac users.

Figure 5.22

.Mac offers a powerful set of useful Internet features.

Choose a Web-page style

Start by opening iWeb. When it opens, you get a screen that asks you to choose a template for your Web page (**Figure 5.23**).

Figure 5.23

Pick a style that suits your tastes.

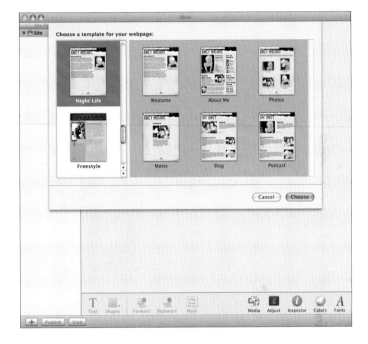

An even dozen styles of templates are available; keep in mind that the templates can be changed radically, if you so desire. Each of these 12 templates has 6 prefabricated pages: Welcome, About Me, Photos, Movie, Blog, and Podcast. For the sake of simplicity (and because you're reading a podcasting book), choose the Podcast template.

Create the Entries page

This part is very easy. Start by clicking Entries in the Site Organizer on the left side of the iWeb screen. The various fields in the Entries page you selected are filled with gibberish or other placeholder text. Simply click the area you want to change, and enter your own information.

Change the title and the description of the podcast, and of course, you also want to insert a picture for your podcast (**Figure 5.24**). You can accomplish this simply by dragging a picture into the template.

Figure 5.24

Find the picture you want to put on the page, and simply drag it over. You can drag directly from your Mac Desktop to the Web page.

When the picture is in place and the text is written (**Figure 5.25**), the Entries page is ready to go except for the podcast itself.

Figure 5.25

The Entries page lists the most recent podcasts (if any).

To add the podcast, click the Media button at the bottom of the iWeb window to display the Media Browser; then click the Audio button at the top of the Media Browser, and select iTunes in the top pane to see a list of MP3 or AAC files in your iTunes library. Select your podcast, which I assume is already in your iTunes library (**Figure 5.26**). When the podcast is in place, you're ready to move to the Podcast page.

Figure 5.26

Select your podcast in the iTunes library.

Create the Podcast page

Back in iWeb, click Podcast in the Site Organizer on the left side of the window to open the Podcast page. The Podcast page is the main page, so it contains information such as the name of the podcast, the byline of the podcast, and the descriptive text (**Figure 5.27**). Again, the template has gibberish or placeholder text that you can simply click to change. Type the information you want, and a very straightforward two-page podcasting site is ready to go.

Figure 5.27

The Podcast page contains important information such as the byline of your podcast, your name, and the name of the podcast series.

Publish the podcast to the iTunes Podcast Directory

When the pages are ready, you can send the podcast to the iTunes Podcast Directory by choosing File > Submit Podcast to iTunes (**Figure 5.28**). When you do this, you immediately get a warning about content rights (**Figure 5.29**), advising you that you are not to use any music or other materials that are copyrighted (unless you have permission to do so).

Figure 5.28

Choose File > Submit Podcast to iTunes.

Figure 5.29

You are warned not to use copyrighted material.

Next up, you need to enter your copyright information (**Figure 5.30**), sign in with your .Mac address or Apple ID (**Figure 5.31**), formally submit the podcast to iTunes (**Figure 5.32**), wait for the podcast to upload, and then review the podcast information (**Figure 5.33**). When all this is done, the process is complete, and your podcast goes into queue for review by the powers that be at Apple. If it passes muster, the podcast appears in the directory within a few days!

Figure 5.30

Enter your copyright information.

Figure 5.31

Sign in with your .Mac address or Apple ID.

Figure 5.32

Submit the podcast to the iTunes directory, and wait for it to upload.

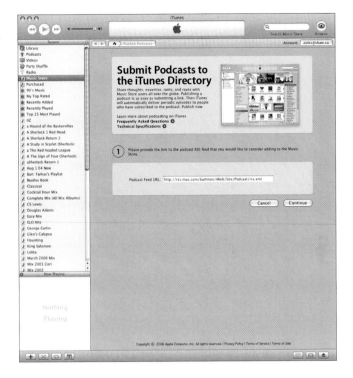

Figure 5.33

Look over the final information before completing the process.

Web-Site Packagers

If creating your own Web site and managing RSS files are things you would rather not do, several online options can ease the pain of learning RSS. Web-site packagers (as I call them) offer up complete packages for hosting an RSS feed so that your podcasts can be available to the masses with little effort on your part. The rub, of course, is that most of these Web sites charge a fee for this service.

This section looks at four Web-site packagers that offer services enabling you to get your podcast and site up and running in a very short period with relatively little blood, sweat, and tears. This field is changing so rapidly that a search on Google is likely to yield a large number of companies willing to host your podcasts.

Liberated Syndication

Liberated Syndication (www.libsyn.com; **Figure 5.34**) is a Web hosting company designed specifically for podcasting. Libsyn.com goes beyond simple Web-site hosting; it offers a podcast-specific product that includes storage for media (podcasts) and an easy-to-use interface for publishing your podcast.

Although Liberated Syndication doesn't offer a front-end Web page per se, it does offer an easy solution for publishing your podcast to an RSS feed for a relatively low cost. The costs of the company's services range from $5 per month (100 MB of storage space) to $30 per month (800 MB). Liberated Syndication takes the attitude that it doesn't want users to be penalized if their programs become popular. Therefore, it does not charge for bandwidth use—only for the space that users' podcasts take up on its servers.

Liberated Syndication is my No. 1 choice for this sort of service. The prices are *very* reasonable, and you would be hard pressed to find another service that offers so much for so little.

Figure 5.34

Liberated Syndication is an excellent Web-hosting service that's dedicated to podcasters.

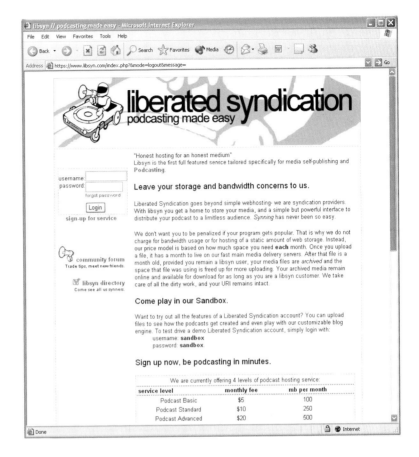

The list of features, as noted on the Libsyn.com Web site, are as follows:

- Unmetered bandwidth

- Easy-to-use interface

- No lock-in (users are not tied to Libsyn.com for their podcasting needs)

- Quickcast feature that immediately creates a podcast feed for an uploaded media file

MyPodcasts.net

MyPodcasts.net (www.mypodcasts.net; **Figure 5.35**) is a podcast management, hosting, and distribution solution that gets your podcast out to the world for $9.99 per month. MyPodcasts.net also includes a set of controls and statistics that tell you exactly how many times your podcast has been downloaded and how many times your RSS feed has been subscribed to. This is a very handy Web site that includes all the tools and tutorials you need to get your podcast distributed around the 'net (including in the iTunes directory).

Figure 5.35

MyPodcasts.net is a podcast Web page/distribution solution.

Podblaze

Podblaze (www.podblaze.com; **Figure 5.36**) is a podcast distribution Web site that takes you through the steps of getting your podcast out onto the Internet in a few short minutes. Podblaze charges various amounts of money, depending on the amount of storage you want for your podcast, but the basic subscription (which includes 200 MB of storage space and 2 GB of bandwidth) is $14.95 per month or $160 per year. Podblaze offers several extra features, including a guarantee that your podcasts will be available in Google searches within 72 hours.

Figure 5.36

Podblaze is a podcast distribution tool that will store your podcasts and distribute them (including getting them on Google) for a fee.

Podbus.com

Podbus.com (www.podbus.com; **Figure 5.37**) is another outstanding commercial Web-hosting service for podcasters. For only $5 a month, Podbus offers 300 MB of storage space and 10 GB of bandwidth. Additionally, if you happen to exceed the 10 GB bandwidth limit, additional bandwidth costs just 66 cents per gigabyte.

Figure 5.37

Podbus.com is an outstanding service for hosting podcast feeds.

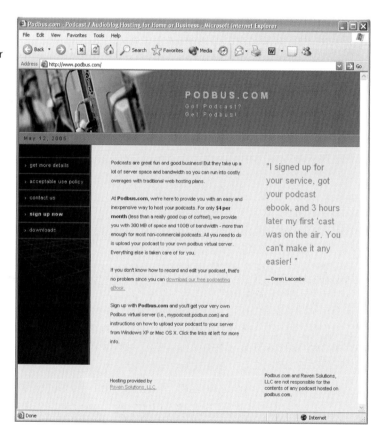

Podbus also includes automatic RSS feed creation. In other words, when a podcast is added to its server, a podcast feed is generated automatically (saving you the pain and suffering of creating your own). The one thing Podbus.com offers that Libsyn.com does not is Web hosting. For a measly $2 per month, Podbus.com allows you to use your 300 MB of space to host your own Web page.

The Podcasting Community at Work

I can imagine a world in which everyone thinks of podcasters as nerds with poor social skills, but this story from Swoopy, co-host of "Skepticality," shows us that the podcasting community really is a community that cares.

On September 8, 2005, Derek Colanduno (**Figure 5.38**) had a stroke. Oddly enough, that was the very day that we had received word that Steve Jobs had included us among the nine most popular podcasts—alongside CNN and ABC News and Adam Curry—on iTunes and had shown our logo on a huge screen during his most recent Apple keynote address.

Figure 5.38
Derek Colanduno, who suffered a stroke at age 31.

Over the past nearly seven months, Derek has worked tirelessly to regain his physical stamina and abilities, as well as learning again how to speak and write, and regain most of his cognitive skills.

Podcasting has been an excellent tool, not only for his therapists to have an idea of the way Derek was like before the stroke, but especially in hearing the way he used to speak. Also, for Derek to be able to record himself speaking and hear the differences in his speech has been extremely helpful in his ongoing recovery.

Although Derek's stroke has changed our lives in many ways, some of the biggest surprises came from the outreach of the podcasting community. The night that Derek had his stroke, I knew that I had to let a lot of people know (because most of our friends are podcasters who listen to our show, and vice versa) what had happened, and an e-mail just seemed beyond me at the time. So I sat down and recorded a short podcast that I called "The Message."

Practically overnight, I was flooded with thousands of e-mails of condolence, well wishes, prayers (even tongue-in-cheek ones), and offers of support of just about every kind, from medical to monetary. Adam Curry replayed my message a couple of days later on "Daily Source Code," and more and more messages continued to pour in, along with flowers, gift baskets, and lots and lots of get-well cards from people we'd never met or never heard from before.

The podcasting community last September was probably a quarter of the size that it is now, and to get that kind of heartfelt outpouring really demonstrated what a special breed of people it was that had created this new kind of media format.

A Talk with Swoopy of "Skepticality"

"Skepticality" (www.skepticality.com; **Figure 5.39**) caters to those among us who are skeptical in nature—that is, those of us who want actual proof that UFOs exist, not just anecdotes from people who say that they've been abducted. It has the distinction of having been listed as one of Steve Jobs's favorite podcasts, so its place in the iTunes directory is secure (just kidding).

Figure 5.39

"Skepticality" has the distinction of being one of Steve Jobs's favorite podcasts.

Swoopy is the co-host of "Skepticality."

Farkas: What was the genesis of "Skepticality"? Whose idea was it, and what were the hurdles in getting things rolling?

Swoopy: "Skepticality" was all Derek's idea. In early 2005, our tiny company, Batpig Studios, was just about to begin shooting footage for an instructional DVD we were working on. Derek was doing some research on audio equipment and setups, and came across a Web site for a podcast called "The Point." He delved into the forums and began having conversations with Paul Figgiani, a fantastically talented audio engineer and producer of "The Point." That was how Derek discovered podcasting, and he began his campaign to bug me about doing one of our own until I relented.

The next hurdle was to figure out what this podcasting thing was and how to go about it. We had all the equipment already; in fact, we were way ahead of the curve there. All that was left was the topic. The standard "he said, she said" format didn't interest us. What we noticed, though, was a lack of topics that we found truly interesting: the stuff that we talked about late into the night over greasy food at our favorite hangout and the stuff that caused deep discussion and often debate. Science, of course. Science, critical thinking, and the lack thereof in the world we live in.

Farkas: What's the mission of "Skepticality"?

Swoopy: We're striving for nothing less than total universal domination. Actually, all we want is to make people think, and more than that, for people to think for themselves and look at the world around them in a more critical way. While some of the sexy topics of skepticism, like the paranormal and all the fun that goes with that, are very entertaining, some very down-to-earth things that we deal with in day-to-day life, beg for the same kind of litmus test.

Farkas: In terms of skepticism, what brought you to this position?

Swoopy: Derek has been a lifelong skeptic, and that is definitely something that is a product of the environment he grew up in and the way his parents raised him. I, on the other hand, am the epitome of a late bloomer. While my worldview and Derek's have always been on fairly level ground, I am usually the first one to present the possibility that there could be another side to his classical point of view.

Farkas: What was it like to be one of Steve Jobs's top podcasts? Did you feel that it validated your hard work?

Swoopy: It was, and is, one of the coolest things that has ever happened and probably will ever happen. While it was a huge source of personal satisfaction, the better part was the sense that we were raising the volume of the voice that belongs to a group of people who really aren't heard loudly enough.

What it really meant to us was that critical thinking—and people who love science and think that common sense and skepticism are important—were definitely out there, and that they were listening, and we were going to be, at least in this small way, counted.

Farkas: Why is podcasting important in the 21st century?

Swoopy: As the mass media finds more and more ways to infiltrate our every day life (who knew we'd have to watch Coca-Cola commercials at the movies, when we're already there drinking soda anyway?), the much-lauded voice of the "everyman" gets lost.

Podcasting is the ultimate way to make oneself heard. And while the mass media is spending revolting amounts of money to tell people what they should eat, listen to, and wear—how to live their lives so that they fit in (to a box no one really wants to be in anyway)—podcasters in their basements are creating content for a generation of people who truly want to pick and choose their media very selectively, and they are doing it for next to nothing.

Farkas: What place does video podcasting have in the podcasting realm?

Swoopy: For content that is enhanced by visuals, it's definitely a cool thing. As independent film was to big studio moviemaking, I think video podcasting can be for television. It's on-demand and available on portable devices. That's exactly what people are looking for. And it's the ultimate in reality television, and we all know how popular that is.

I don't think, however, that videoblogging, vlogging, or video podcasting will do anything to diminish the importance or popularity of podcasting among the audience it was originally intended for. The benefit of audio programming is that it is passive. You can listen to podcasts while doing almost any activity. Watching video requires you to be paying attention to it, and that rules out a lot of activities, like driving and such.

Also, when you present your audience all the visuals, you lose the "theater of the mind" appeal that pure audio can provide. Sometimes, your own imagination is better than any video. Everyone who has had a favorite book turned into a lackluster movie knows what that's like.

R
A
m
b
e
a
u,
Benjamin
3/27

Benjamin

3/27

A

Resources

Podcasting as a known entity is not even 2 years old, yet in this very short time, it has already woven its way into the world's consciousness, vernacular, and commerce channels. Podcasting as an entity is progressing and changing at a blinding pace. Heck, even between the first and second editions of this book, much has changed—case in point, the arrival of video podcasting on the scene. This breakneck speed is partially because of the nature of the Internet and partially because podcasting is a new medium that is still finding its niche in society.

Because of the ever-changing nature of this medium, I recommend that you check out www.peachpit.com/podcasting to get updates on the most up-to-date Web sites and resources available. Despite the continual morphing of the podcasting realm, there is a large number of important Web sites that I'd be remiss if I didn't mention.

Podcasting-Related Web Sites

This section includes links to Web sites relating to podcasting as an entity. These sites provide information about the community, as well as links to software and podcasts. These are the first sites that a new podcaster should visit to get a feel for the community.

Our podcast

To listen to the podcast made especially for this book, check out this site:

www.peachpit.com/podcasting

General podcasting Web sites

These Web sites are catch-all reservoirs of podcasting information. Most of these sites contain how-to information, a top-ten list of podcasts, a large bank of podcast feeds, and links to the latest and greatest software for podcasting-related activities.

Digital Media Tips N Tricks (video podcasting): www.codedsignal.com/serendipity

iPodder.org: www.ipodder.org

Podblaze: www.podblaze.com

Podcast Alley: www.podcastalley.com

Podcast Bunker: www.podcastbunker.com

Podcast Central: www.podcastcentral.com

Podcast Expert at Podcast and Portable Expo: www.portablemediaexpo.com/podcastexpert/index.php

Podcast.net: www.podcast.net

The Podcast Network: www.thepodcastnetwork.com

Podcasting News: www.podcastingnews.com

Podcasting Tools: www.podcasting-tools.com

The School of Podcasting: www.schoolofpodcasting.com

Weblogs.com: http://audio.weblogs.com

General search engines

These are the search engines you can use to scour the World Wide Web for anything related to podcasting. These engines gather data by the minute, so making the same search every day or so often yields different results.

AltaVista: www.altavista.com

Ask.com: www.ask.com

Google: www.google.com

Lycos: www.lycos.com

MSN: www.msn.com

Yahoo!: www.yahoo.com

Podcast search engines

Although any search engine, such as Yahoo! or Google, can come up with all things podcasting, only one (Podscope) currently is dedicated to searching for specific words or phrases *in* podcasts themselves.

Feedster.com: www.feedster.com

Podcast Directory: www.podcastdirectory.com

Podcast.net: www.podcast.net

The Podcast Network: www.thepodcastnetwork.com

Podscope: www.podscope.com

Yahoo! Podcasts: http://podcasts.yahoo.com

Podcasting-related sites

These Web sites are not catch-all podcasting sites, but they often contain valuable information for some topic related to podcasting.

Engadget: www.engadget.com

Podcast and Portable Media Expo: www.portablemediaexpo.com

Podcasting Avenue: http://podcasters.blogspot.com

Really Simple Syndication Web sites (RSS)

These Web sites cover everything from the history of RSS to the down-and-dirty details of the specification itself.

Berkman Center for Internet & Society (Harvard University): http://blogs.law.harvard.edu/tech/rss

RSS Digest: www.bigbold.com/rssdigest

Music legalities

These are the various Web sites where Creative Commons–licensed music is available and where you can learn about Creative Commons. I have also included the license links for both ASCAP and BMI.

ASCAP Internet Music License Agreements: www.ascap.com/weblicense

BMI Web Site Music Performance Agreement: www.bmi.com/licensing/forms/Internet0105A.pdf

Creative Commons: http://creativecommons.org

The Freesound Project: http://freesound.iua.upf.edu/index.php

Opsound: www.opsound.com

Podcasting software: aggregators (podcatchers)

These are the programs that go out and grab the podcasts for you to listen to. Some of the podcast aggregators listed here are not covered in this book, but I thought it worthwhile to list them here for your convenience.

Armangil's podcatcher: http://podcatcher.rubyforge.org

BashPodder: http://linc.homeunix.org:8080/scripts/bashpodder

CastGrab: http://castgrab.berlios.de

Doppler: www.dopplerradio.net

FeedDemon: www.newsgator.com/NGOLProduct.aspx?ProdId=FeedDemon

FeederReader: www.feederreader.com

Golden Ear: http://brooklynnorth.com

HappyFish: http://thirstycrow.net/happyfish/default.aspx

iPodder: www.ipodder.org

iPodder.NET: http://ipoddernet.sourceforge.net

iTunes 6: www.apple.com/itunes

jPodder: www.jpodder.com

Nimiq: www.nimiq.nl

Now Playing: http://brandon.fuller.name/archives/hacks/nowplaying

PlayPod: www.iggsoftware.com/playpod/index.html

PocketRSS: www.happyjackroad.net/pocketpc/pocketRSS/pocketRSS.asp

Podcast Tuner: http://thenowhereman.com/podcasttuner

PodOmatic: www.podomatic.com/home

Pod2Go: www.kainjow.com/pod2go

ppcTunes: www.pocketmac.net/products/ppctunes

Primetime Podcast Receiver: www.primetimepodcast.com

RSSRadio: www.dorada.co.uk

Synclosure: http://raphb.ch/c/synclosure

Transistr (formerly iPodderX): http://transistr.com

TVTonic: www.tvtonic.com

WinPodder: www.winpodder.com

Podcasting software: creating podcasts

This is the software that you use to create podcasts from scratch. From recording the content to editing out mistakes and inserting music, these are the programs that do it.

Adobe Audition 2.0: www.adobe.com/products/audition

Audacity: http://audacity.sourceforge.net/download

Audio Hijack: www.rogueamoeba.com/audiohijack

CastBlaster: www.castblaster.com

Digidesign Pro Tools LE: www.digidesign.com

Easy Hi-Q Recorder: www.roemersoftware.com/moreinfo5.html

ePodcast Producer: www.industrialaudiosoftware.com/products/epodcastproducer.html

GarageBand: www.apple.com/garageband

Jazler Radio Automation: www.jazler.com/products/jazlerradio.asp

MixCast Live: www.mixcastlive.com

Panorama: http://wavearts.com/Panorama5.html

PodProducer: www.podproducer.net

Propaganda: www.makepropaganda.com

Sound Byte: www.blackcatsystems.com/software/soundbyte.html

SoundEdit Pro: www.rmbsoft.com/sep.asp

Sound Forge: www.sonymediasoftware.com/products

Sound Recorder (Windows): www.microsoft.com

Sparks! 2.0: www.blogmatrix.com/products/main

Podcasting software: publishing podcasts

These are the links for the software packages I've recommended that can help you create an RSS feed with ease.

ePodcast Producer: www.industrialaudiosoftware.com/products/epodcastproducer.html

Feed Editor: www.extralabs.net/feed-editor.htm

Feeder: www.reinventedsoftware.com

FeedForAll: www.feedforall.com

Live365 (streaming): www.live365.com/index.live

Nicecast (streaming): www.rogueamoeba.com/nicecast

PodShock: www.podshock.com

Propaganda: www.makepropaganda.com

Sparks! 2.0: www.blogmatrix.com/products/main

Widget Podcast: www.widgetpodcast.com

Publishing podcasts: Web-site hosting solutions

These are sites I recommend if you are interested in paying a hosting service that specializes in podcasts to host your files.

Liberated Syndication: www.libsyn.com

MediaBlog: http://mediablog.mail2web.com

MyPodcasts.net: www.mypodcasts.net

Podbus.com: www.podbus.com

PodshowCreator: www.podshowcreator.com

Switchpod: http://switchpod.com

WebCyberHosting: www.webcyberhosting.com

Commercial podcast sources

I can't possibly list every commercial venture that has podcasts available. That said, these are the major sites that you can visit just to get
the flavor of what's available.

Audible.com: www.audible.com

AudioBooksForFree.com: www.audiobooksforfree.com

Audiobooks Online: www.audiobooksonline.com

Blackstone Audiobooks: www.blackstoneaudio.com

CBC.ca (Canadian Broadcasting Corporation): www.cbc.ca

ESPN: http://espnradio.espn.go.com/espnradio/podcast/index

iTunes Music Store: www.apple.com/itunes/store

National Public Radio: www.npr.org

Other software

These are links to software that can play a role in podcasting, from
media players to Web-page design programs.

Dreamweaver: www.macromedia.com/software/dreamweaver

FrontPage: www.microsoft.com

 **Microsoft is phasing out FrontPage,
but it's still in broad use.**

GoLive: www.adobe.com/products/golive/main.html

QuickTime: www.apple.com/quicktime

RealPlayer: www.real.com

Replay Radio: www.applian.com/replay-radio/index.php

Windows Media Player: www.microsoft.com

Top podcasts

To come up with this list, I went to Podcast Alley and took the top 15 podcasts from its voted top-50 list one day in April 2006.

1. "MuggleCast": www.mugglecast.com

2. "Free Talk Live": http://freetalklive.com

3. "Science Talk: The Podcast of *Scientific American* Magazine": www.sciam.com/podcast

4. "The Dawn and Drew Show": http://dawnanddrew.podshow.com

5. "Keith and The Girl": http://keithandthegirl.com

6. "Slacker Astronomy": www.slackerastronomy.com/wordpress/index.php

7. "The MacCast": www.maccast.com

8. "Daily Breakfast": www.sqpn.com/scripts/dailybreakfast.php

9. "Coverville": www.coverville.com

10. "Geek News Central": www.geeknewscentral.com

11. "Comic Geek Speak": http://comicgeekspeak.blogspot.com

12. "Slice of Sci-Fi": http://sliceofscifi.com

13. "Skepticality": www.skepticality.com

14. "The Bob and AJ Show": www.bobandaj.info

15. "Soccergirl, Incorporated": http://soccergirl.podshow.com

Hardware

These links take you to companies that manufacture some of the hardware discussed in this book.

Apple Computer: www.apple.com

Audio-Technica: www.audiotechnica.com

Behringer: www.behringer.com

COWON America: http://eng.cowon.com

Creative: www.creative.com

Edirol: www.edirol.com

Electrovoice: www.electrovoice.com

Griffin Technology: www.griffintechnology.com

iRiver: www.iriver.com

JVC: www.jvc.com

Labtec: www.labtec.com

Logitech: www.logitech.com

Marantz: www.marantz.com

M-Audio: www.m-audio.com

Rio Audio: www.digitalnetworksna.com/rioaudio

Sony: www.sony.com

Other interesting sites

This section lists other interesting Web sites that are related to podcasts and/or podcasting in some way.

Duke Digital Initiative: www.duke.edu/ddi

How-To Podcasting: www.engadget.com/entry/5843952395227141

TVTonic: www.tvtonic.com

Veoh: www.veoh.com

Glossary

You may not be familiar with some terms mentioned in this book. Although many of these terms will be familiar to those who have experience with the World Wide Web, some terminology may be confusing to newcomers. This glossary should clear up any confusion.

A

AAC: Stands for *Advanced Audio Coding,* a type of digital compression that is used to reduce the size of music files while maintaining quality. AAC, which is the preferred method of digital encoding for Apple Computer and its line of iPod players, is superior in quality to the MP3 format but still part of the MPEG specification. *See also* MPEG, MP3.

ActiveSync: A program from Microsoft that synchronizes data between a PC and portable devices running the Windows Mobile or Windows CE operating system.

aggregator: A piece of software that scours specific areas on the World Wide Web to find selected content and then deliver it to your computer.

audio blog: A Web log (blog) that contains audio files instead of written text.

B

bit rate: The speed at which bits of data flow through a specific area or connection. The bit rate measures the number of bits over time (bits per second).

BitTorrent: A peer-to-peer file distribution program. Files are broken into smaller chunks, distributed in fragments, and then reassembled on the requesting machine. If a piece is missing, each peer takes advantage of the best connection to find the missing pieces. BitTorrent is an effective tool for sharing large amounts of data, such as videos and large audio files. *See also* peer-to-peer.

blog: A term formed by the combination of the words *Web* and *log*. A blog is a Web-based page where content is added periodically. The content of a blog can range from diary entries to news items to podcasts.

blogging: The act of contributing to or running a Web log (blog). Depending on the form of the blog, there can be various incarnations of the name, including video blogging, audio blogging, and photo blogging.

C

CPU: Stands for *central processing unit*, the brains of a computer.

D

digital media device: Any hard drive– or flash memory–based device capable of playing media such as music, video, and podcasts.

digital music device: Any hard drive– or flash memory–based digital music player. *See also* hard-drive memory, flash memory.

F

flash memory: A kind of RAM (Random Access Memory) that does not lose the data it contains when the power on the device is turned off. Flash memory is limited by the size of the chip and generally is a fraction of the space available on a hard drive.

flash player: An MP3 player that uses flash memory to hold information.

FTP: Stands for *File Transfer Protocol,* a protocol for transferring large files over the Internet.

H

hard-drive memory: A digital memory medium using a hard drive. In the context of digital music devices, hard drives are not unlike the hard drives used in your home computer. The most significant difference between these hard drives is the size; hard drives in digital music players can be as small as a stack of three quarters!

hyperlink: A word or string of words in a document linking to another resource, such as a Web page or another document.

I

iPod: A hard drive– or flash memory–based digital media player from Apple Computer, Inc.

iTunes: Apple's Mac- and PC-based software for managing MP3s, AAC files, and other audio content among the World Wide Web, your computer, and your iPod.

L

LCD: Stands for *liquid crystal display,* the type of screen used in many digital media players.

M

MPEG: Stands for *Moving Pictures Expert Group,* a digital information compression standard that allows large digital files, such as audio and video files, to be compressed nearly tenfold without much quality loss. *See also* MP3.

MP3: A type of digital compression that is used to reduce the size of music files while maintaining quality. MP3 compression is part of MPEG compression.

N

newbie: Slang for someone who is new to a particular concept or discipline.

O

Ogg Vorbis: An open-source file compression format, similar to MP3.

OOG: *See* Ogg Vorbis.

OPML: Stands for *Outline Processor Markup Language,* a kind of programming language that is used to create files for Really Simple Syndication (RSS).

P

peer-to-peer: A computer network that uses the computers on the "edges" of the network rather than a central point or the network itself. In short, peer-to-peer takes advantage of all the computers on the network to speed things up.

plug-in: A piece of software that can be "plugged" into an existing program to modify it in some way.

podcast: A digital broadcast that can be loaded onto a digital music device, such as an MP3 player.

podcatcher: A piece of software (also known as an *aggregator*) that goes out on the Internet and finds podcasts for download.

podwaves: An analog to airwaves.

preamp: Stands for *preamplifier,* an amplifier that comes before another amplifier. In the case of podcasting, the preamp usually powers the microphone.

P2P: *See* peer-to-peer.

R

RAM: Stands for *Random Access Memory,* a computer-chip form of memory. Information such as computer programs and data is temporarily stored in RAM while the computer is turned on. As a general rule, RAM is volatile memory, and its contents are lost when power is removed. Flash memory is an exception to this rule.

RSS: Stands for *Really Simple Syndication*, a protocol designed to make it easy for the average person to get podcasts out for the world to hear.

RSS feed: The actual link to the podcast or other file to be syndicated.

S

streaming media: A form of broadcasting in which content is streamed directly from a Web site to a home computer. This content is played "live" on the computer as it is streamed rather than being saved on the computer's hard drive.

U

URL: Stands for *Uniform Resource Locator*, the address of a Web page, often starting with www.

USB: Stands for *Universal Serial Bus*, a now-standard connection modality for PCs and Macs.

USB 2.0: A much faster form of the USB bus.

V

video podcast: A podcast broadcast in video format.

vlog: A blog (Web log) in video format.

vodcasting: A synonym for video podcasting.

W

WAV: Stands for *WAVEform*, Microsoft's audio format.

Webcasting: A form of broadcasting in which the content is downloaded directly off a Web site to a home computer and onto the computer's hard drive.

Web log: *See* blog.

X

XML: Stands for *Extensible Markup Language*, a programming language that underpins RSS.

Index

Web sites *(continued)*
    Canadian Broadcasting Corporation (CBC), 59
    creating for podcast storage, 229
    Creative, 85
    Creative Commons, 140
    eZedia, 189
    FeederReader, 22
    FeedForAll, 252
    GeeThree, 189
    Griffin Technology, 9
    HappyJackRoad, 34
    iPodder, 24
    iPodder.NET, 26–27
    iRiver, 84
    KYOU Radio, 63
    Live365, 247
    Logitech, 103
    Magix, 124
    NPR (National Public Radio), 65
    Opsound, 141
    packagers
        Liberated Syndication, 264–265
        MyPodcasts.net, 266
        Podblaze, 267
        Podbus.com, 268
    Peachpit Press, 276
    Podcast Alley, 3, 239
    Podcast Bunker, 239
    podcasting availability, 7–8
    Podcasting News, 239
    PoddumFeeder, 35
    Propaganda, 254
    Radio Shack, 104
    RealPlayer, 76
    Reinvented Software, 251
    Replay Radio, 62
    resources, 276
        aggregator sites, 279–280
        book podcast, 277
        commercial podcasts, 282
        general Web sites, 277–278
        hardware, 284
        music legalities, 278
        publishing software sites, 281
        RSS (Really Simple Syndication) sites, 278
        search engines, 278
        software, 280–283

    top podcasts, 283
    Web site hosting solutions, 281–282
    Sirius Radio, 57
    Stupendous Software, 189
    Thirsty Crow, 23
    Tree House Concerts, 6
    TVTonic, 41
    XM Satellite Radio, 57
Weblogs.com, marketing podcast, 238
Williams, Ben, interview, 184–185
Williams, Robin, Audible.com show, 52
Winder, Dave, RSS (Really Simple Syndication), 228
Windows Media Player (WMP), watching video podcasts, 177
Windows PCs
    capturing podcasts, 21
        HappyFish, 47–48
    creating podcasts tutorial
        connecting equipment, 152–153
        editing vocal content, 160–161
        exporting to MP3 format, 164–165
        finishing touches, 162–163
        recording podcast, 158–159
        software configuration, 154–157
    creating video podcast tutorial
        adding digital effects, 200–201
        adjusting audio levels, 203–204
        audio import, 197–198
        connecting equipment, 192–193
        dragging clips into timeline, 199
        importing video into software, 195–196
        inserting transitions, 202
        powering up camcorder, 194
        saving and exporting to Web, 204–205
WMP (Windows Media Player), playing podcasts, 77

X–Y–Z